Rhetoric, Rhymes and Rants

Michael Brown
(aka embi, Greywolf, Light Brown)

Zen Doodles by June Tokuyama-Brown
Cover Artwork by Tony Guaraldi-Brown

ISBN: 1492213519
ISBN-13: 978-1492213512

DEDICATION

This is dedicated to the one I love,
my courageous and dedicated wife, June.

Happy Holidays,
Justine, Kevin, Grace + Rylan!

Lots of love,
Chimène, John ♡
Jasper + Kiana

Xmas 2014

3

ACKNOWLEDGMENTS

Without the loving assistance of my brother, Harold Merlin Brown, his erudite wife, Davida Jean Brown, and my generous friend and advisor, John Lee, this book would not have happened. I wish to thank Tony Guaraldi-Brown for his generosity with his wondrous artwork, re: my book cover, and my lovely wife June Tokuyama-Brown for her inspired zen doodles for each chapter. I wish to thank Tom Ellis for the artwork on my CD cover. I wish to thank Eli Brown for his insightful and heartfelt introduction. I wish to thank David for his foreword and for being a unique and wonderful friend, who never quit and manages to stay in "touch" every single day! Thanks for being there and here. Finally, my special thanks to my Men's Team for their continued support of me and my wife.

INTRODUCTION AND FOREWORD

Introduction by Eli Brown

Author of *Cinnamon and Gunpowder*

The book is arranged like a scrapbook. Or rather, it is a shoebox of memorabilia, entire eras tied together with string.

Whether reading straight through, or drifting from one poem to another, we hear not one voice, but a chorus of whispers. The box suddenly seems deeper than it first looked. The images unfold and are seen, pages later from a different angle. Another hand seems to be sifting through with us, and another. Old lovers, lost friends, lessons learned so early they feel biblical, they're all here. The signposts misled us; here is a love song listed under Life Sentence and a screeching collision under Portraits. Suddenly the box is bigger than the room. We're lost.

Walt Whitman also had this kind of licentious messiness, this open-door-policy that lets ghosts and nudes and wizards wander through. It must be the result of a mind that does not reject anything immediately but watches to learn if there is something good in it. The builder sees a knot in the wood as an embellishment; the cook knows what can be done with bitter kale; the musician hears a rhythm in the racket. Couched between dense lyrics, for example, Attendant's Smile is a piece of found art, a script for a bedside dialogue, apparently saved verbatim because it was perfect just as it was.

Like Sharon Olds, and Rukeyser before her, Brown makes no apology for what monsters we might stumble upon. There is a wolf in these pages and we can hear it gnawing. Don't trust it to stay in behind the fence of Life Sentence. It knows whose woods these are.

The poems that chronicle the cruel progression of disease and assaults on dignity read like Dante's progression into hell itself. They are letters from the edge and seem to say, You will not believe what I have seen here in the trenches, but I will tell you anyway...

In Resurrection, (For June) Brown seems to be describing his own reanimation from a deathlike coma, pulled back into being itself by the image and love of his wife. It reminds us of the myth of Orpheus (who was also a musician) only in reverse. His longing for her is so primal and plaintive, it is as if death had nearly claimed her instead of him. In its whittled-to-the-bone form, the poem echoes the eighteenth century haiku master Buson whose poem about a widower is similarly cutting:

The piercing chill I feel:

My dead wife's comb, in our bedroom,

under my heel

Resurrection, for me, is the beating heart of the book. It is a dirge that transcends the individual and cries out for life itself.

But Brown's adoration for other elements of this world are no less vivid. In 24/7/365 he longs for a sunburn, for example, which is something we might expect only love-drunk Rumi to want. And in Lyrrin he swoons over an infant's smile:

I like

hanging out

on the corners

of your mouth.

In the darkness he has provided light. Babies run babbling through these woods providing a hope and joy long after their actual influences have grown to adulthood. Yes, the wolf is among us but there are so very many of us, and more on the way. It's hard to be afraid with company like this.

Singer turns breath into song, carpenter turns a tree into a home, cook turns the scattered pieces of the world into food. With these poems, Brown has managed a deeper transformation. He has turned grief into wisdom, trouble into beauty. He has lived a life.

Foreword by Dave Clarke

Author of *Keeping Hannah Waiting*

Michael and I came to be friends by a quirk of fate.

When we met, he was working as a chef. I soon came to know him as a sawyer and a miller and I had the pleasure and good fortune of working alongside him in the redwood forests of the Santa Cruz Mountains learning how to turn fallen timber into workable lumber.

Whenever we were to meet – at a job site, at my house, at his house – Michael was always there ahead of me, waiting in his truck, a paperback police procedural or spy thriller in his hands, and a warm "Hey, you…" to greet me.

Over time, I also came to know him as a musician, a lyricist, a composer, a singer, an actor, a carpenter, a builder, a fixer of things, a patient student and an even more-patient teacher, and most of all as a friend.

During our countless hours conversing over sawdust and sandwiches, he never failed to surprise me by choosing the right word to describe something, the perfect word for the job, as if he were pulling another tool out of his tool box, a tool designed for a specific purpose.

It comes as no surprise to me then that this, a compilation of his many words and thoughts, is also full of the right words to sum up a lifetime of highs and lows, good times and bad, the little things in life that pick us up and sometimes, the big things that bring us down.

So, take the time to ruminate on his rhetoric, revel in his rhymes, and relish his rants. You're certain to find something to savor throughout.

And to you, Michael, I say "Hey, you" right back atcha. Thanks for being my friend.

SONG LYRICS

GREYWOLF

MICHAEL BENJAMIN BROWN

June's Song

Verse:
It's the simple things we know and love
that can never be put down
like your laughter on the wind,
So good to know you're still around.

I'm so grateful for my time with you,
you've given me a home.
Now my best friend always rides with me
Even when I walk alone.

First Refrain:
Time and sand I understand
can never stay the same.
Don't waste the wind,
the rain the clouds,
The weather's not to blame.
Time, take the time.
Time, embrace the time,
Time.....

Verse:
I'd sit for hours in the sand
I'd hear the shadows not the sun
while hope was just a ride gone past
without dreams of anyone.

Now I take the time to paint the waves
with music towards the shore
and hold your hopes as if they're mine
I don't know how to love you more.

(Repeat First Refrain)

Verse:
I never dreamed you'd be the gift
we've all been waiting for,
with our together held in place,
teach me how to love you more.

I've given you my time to come
With a promise from the past
It's our word that holds our time in trust
And shares the dream we've built to last

Second Refrain:
Time and sand I understand
can never stay the same.
Forget the sun,
the moon, the tide,
the weather's not to blame.
Time, take the time.
Time, embrace the time,
Time.....

embi 4/2/10

Rainbow Blues

Verse:
You came in like rain in winter
with the passion of a storm.
Found my heart would give you shelter
and my bed would keep you warm.

We found time for love and laughter,
special touching with our hands:
knowing full well that ever after
wasn't really in your plans.

Refrain:
What's the point of chasing rainbows
when the weather doesn't change,
if even love can't teach this ol' fool
to get on in out of the rain?

Verse:
Finding you was like a promise
that the world was right again.
We both knew you'd leave tomorrow.
I just wasn't ready then.

But tomorrow's here and morning's leaving.
You pack the bags, I'll hide the pain.
Standing on the empty sidewalk,
can't tell the teardrops from the rain.

Refrain:
What's the point of chasing rainbows
if the weather doesn't change,
since even love can't teach this ol' fool:
Come on in out of the rain.

But maybe that's the point of chasing rainbows.
I know the treasure's finding you.
If sun and rain can play together,
maybe I'll forget my rainbow blues.

And that's the point of chasing rainbows
since the weather's gonna change.
Cause maybe love can teach this ol' fool:
Come on in out of the rain,
Honey, get your butt on in out of the rain.

embi 8/18/88

Rusty Broken Leaves

Rusty broken leaves
all huddled in a corner
like so many people
afraid of being walked on.

I see back to a time
that can never return
except in sleepless dreams.

My sidewalk mirror fades
as tomorrow is today
leaving a film of regrets
to forget.

I once was
your heart's soul.
Now mine is left as dust,
cornered in
polite recall
as thoughts are made to fall
against your chosen wall,
your wall of will.

How long before we see ourselves
be still and not afraid
of giving time and all its pain,
so wishes can be made to be
and visions know our touch?
You must know I love you very much.

embi 5/9/65

Nightwatch

Verse:
Lying awake near the one that you love
sometimes is a wonderful thing.
Hearing her sounds as she sleeps through the night
I can't tell you the pleasure it brings,
I can't tell you the pleasure it brings.

The lines and the shadows that rest in her smile
as she slumbers with trust in her space,
bring me peace in a world that has frightened my soul,
since I've learned my love's out of place,
since I've learned that my love's out of place.

Bridge:
But there's only the time that we spend with each other,
the rest is illusion we build.
Cause without the time there's only wishes and waste,
and it seems like we're never fulfilled,
yes, it seems like we're never fulfilled.

Now broken pieces of time spill their story too fast.
What we're left with are shadows of us.
Growing old could be fun. We should be proud of our past,
not searching for dreams in the dust,
no, not searching for dreams in the dust.

Verse:
Ah, but love is peculiar, it sometimes brings pain,
and I hurt knowing you hurt inside.
But we know there are flowers that bloom in the rain,
even though on the surface they've died,
even though on the surface they've died.

embi 4/07/83

Indigo Blues

Chorus:
Can I tell you I love you?
Would it be any use?
If we hold our hearts open,
would it stop the abuse?
Please make room on your shoulder.
I'm weary and lost.
You can have my tomorrows;
you're worth more than the cost

Verse:
Cold blues of the night
stacked up to the heavens
with room in our pockets
so we each have our own.
The hues ever-changing
from midnight to dawning.
A purple bruise on the skyline
and my heart heading for home.

My colors of blue
leave me frightened and lonely,
as I watch while your fading,
washed out by the strain.
We both seem to argue
Just to find out who's listening,
unable to honor
each other's pain. (Chorus)

My favorite color
was blue in the morning.
Your eyes seemed to sparkle.
Your smile was the sun.
Where do we gather
the courage to challenge
our errors in judgment
when there's nowhere to run? (Chorus)

Can we bury the weapons
made only for heartache,
and build truth in a promise
so it isn't a lie?
Is there hope under heaven
to create a safe haven --
a place where we both
can see eye to eye? (Chorus)

embi 10/13/10

Country Music Blues

Chorus:
I'll forgive me, you forgive you.
We'll forgive each other, but
the truth is we're through,
we're history, we're history.
Laughter was a sometimes,
stormy silence everyday.
What's wrong with this picture is
it doesn't go away.
We're history, we're history.

The past tense of our marriage
is with us every day,
while I'm looking in your eyes
with nothing left to say.
We try to keep it going
like it's something we should do,
yet each day repeats the pattern:
"Still busy, I'll get back to you." (Chorus)

Barely living in the present,
walking wounded in the past,
still looking for the magic
we both thought would make it last.
Trying to fix a broken record
is a painful way to fail.
We know that living empty
is like dying stuck in jail. (Chorus)

Our thinking has the bad times
worse than none at all,
while our lies and wasted wishes
want the other one to fall.
More alone when we're together;
what's been lost is out of reach.
If we're going to find redemption
we've got to practice what we preach. (Chorus)

embi 4/1/11

Evening Shadows

Chorus:
Evening shadows reach out to carry away
the last desperate remnants of light.
She holds on to the promise that moonlight's a lantern,
to show where he waits in the night.

Verse:
Under cover of darkness lies a rumor of passion,
enfolded in faith like a quilt,
stealing a moment to hold something precious,
blindly donning the mantle of guilt.

Running into disaster only seen from the outside,
too often we reap what we sow.
The cost of the forbidden outweighs the illusion,
that the moment is all that we know.

Now anxiously moving towards imminent sadness,
the joy and the rapture supreme.
Held for a moment, the bliss overwhelming,
transported by love of a dream. (Chorus)

Her family of Nobles made money in shipping,
or so it was said at the time.
But the legends and gossip retold by the frightened,
all speak of their inhuman crimes.

Since no one's been able to capture the creature,
or prove that she even is real.
With her eternal beauty the Shewolf runs freely
with the village still trapped on The WHEEL. (Chorus)

But the wolf knows the story, set free by the moonlight,
engaged in the hunt she must run.
The lover, a young man captured by beauty,
compelled past all reason: UNDONE.

Seen through the forest, he stands like an angel,
waiting for beauty not beast.
The kiss all consuming at the end of the horror,
only one lover left at the feast. (Chorus)

embi 9/11/10

Light'n Up

When you run into trouble,
and you're down on your knees
and the devil is laughin',
doin' what he please,
light'n up. We know, yes, we know.
Right on up, let the light show,
light'n up

If your money is making
a hole in your mind
and your banker says money
is too hard to find,
light'n up. We know, yes, we know.
Right'n up, let the light show,
light'n up.

If your woman is looking at
some other man,
let her know that you love her
as best as you can, and
light'n up. I know, yes, I know.
Right on up, let the light show,
light'n up

We all have our worries,
some even the same.
If we don't help each other,
we have the devil to blame.
Light'n up. We know, yes, we know.
Right on up, let the light show,
light'n up.

Reach out to your neighbor,
take the time, do your part.
When we all work together,
gardens grow in our hearts.
Light'n up. You know, yes, you know.
Right on up. Let your light show.
Light'n up.

embi 5/14/10

FAMILY: GROWING UP

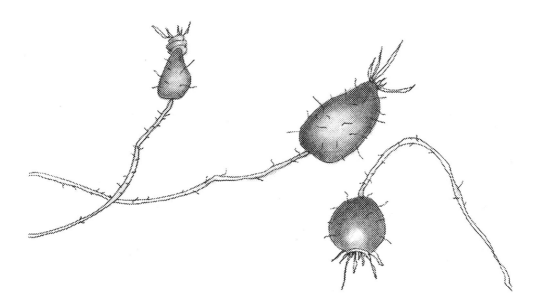

Pop Tarts

(shared morsels with my dad and other family chronicles)

~1~

His den was in the backyard, in the corner by the fence.
He'd disappear for hours, his writings that intense.
Naps were also paramount, us kids would be the clock;
any excuse to go inside, since the door was never locked.
A cot to sleep, a desk to write, a chair to read Shakespeare.
Sometimes he'd let me hold the skull that sat beside his beer.
The floor lamp cast a yellow glow that kept the corners dark.
The Lucky Strikes, the wooden match,
the smell, the smoke, the spark.
Then his one good eye would squint
to keep the smoke from going in.
When he caught me tryin' to steal a sip he couldn't help but grin.
He said to take the can outside and pour it in the ground,
and told me it was full of piss since the bathroom's out of bounds.
Sometimes he'd let me sit beside the lamp in the big chair,
the typewriter would peck away, grey smoke would fill the air.
I'd look at Shakespeare's heroes in a book too big for me.
He'd quote a verse of King Lear's fool,
if that's the picture he could see.
A gift he had, his memory, seemed omnipotent at first.
Now I realize that language was his way to quench his thirst.
The whole back wall of the den was floor to ceiling books,
Faulkner, Steinbeck, Whitehead, Joyce and Saroyan, while the nooks
and crannies held treasures meant to fascinate a boy,
like a gold wrist watch, old fountain pens,
or a cross of Chinese coins.
Outside the den, a garden, where a purple fig tree stood.
The tree was big, so were the figs, besides that they were good!
He'd plant and grow some vegetables, using compost ripe and wet.
Tomatoes, corn, green beans and chard were some of what we'd get.

~2~

We had a St Bernard named Berry, big enough to ride,
which we did from time to time when she'd let us climb her sides.
Sometimes an awkward fall and landing hard enough to hurt;
I'd get a lick from Berry then she'd lift me by my shirt;
if the cry was loud enough and our mom came to the door,
she'd lift me by my collar without tearing what I wore,
and bring me to the back steps so that Mom could check me out;
a hug, some words, a grin, a smile, no time wasted in a pout.
The next adventure, calling for a dog and maybe wheels,
drafting her into service without thinking how she feels.
We were young and she was old, her patience wearing thin,
when she snapped our parents knew it was time to rein us in.
Her leaving left a question mark, like when will she be back,
and where'd she go and is she sad or glad and all of that.
In her passing, we were left without a reason for her death;
which neighbor fed her something that took away her breath,
we'll never really know for sure, just suspicions about who.
But the grace that came so naturally became a thing to do,
whenever certain people's names or bodies came in view.

embi 6/14/11

~3~

Chores with Pop would keep us from the play with other kids,
we'd have to stay til it's done right, until that's what we did.
Sometimes the sacred typewriter would come outside the den,
with a card table, typing paper, a pencil or a pen.
He taught us never to erase, a straight line through would do.
That way the word could still be read as choice against the new.
Another tree of green figs grew in grass we called a lawn.
Our neighbors' yards we'd view by which branch we stood upon.

Our sandbox brought the neighbors cats
and sometimes random dogs.
Mom wasn't really happy when our dump trucks found the "logs."
So my godfather and my dad removed the box and sand,
and built a square cement tub deep enough to stand
up to our waists in water cold enough to chill
the summer's heat while swimming circles, and cannonballs until
shivering and wrinkled blue, Pop's whistle stopped the play,
though we argued through our chattering teeth;
time for dinner anyway.

embi 5/16/11

~4~

Our father dabbled in gourmet, though our mother was the cook.
Both of them were teachers but it wasn't always books.
As brilliant as my father was, we still did things by hand,
like raking leaves and splitting wood and coffee grounds in sand.
His way of teaching showed us how, til correctly done his way:
quality not quantity with results designed to stay.
He built some drawers in our garage for apples, spuds and pears;
produce procurement from those drawers
meant climbing a few stairs.
If he stood at the bottom stair and I the kitchen floor,
then I knew that I could fly through space out the kitchen door.
Trust or faith I don't know which, as children it's just there.
I'd be caught then set down safe, my thoughts still in the air.
Our older sister had first rights at saying what to do,
like when the folks had gone somewhere; their faith in her we knew.
Like water seeks it's own level, I would follow mine.
My kid brother would come along almost all the time.
His faith in me is shocking, now, because we're still alive.
That faith was tested more than once, a wonder we survived.

We had a flexie, we built a ramp, not too steep at first.
Too soon we needed altitude, the woodpile not the worst.
The grape arbor up by the roof, we worked to get it right;
just to get the flexie up, took both stubbornness and might.
When my foot went through the lattice and I fell flat on my back,
the ramp knocked down the woodpile, so now that I had to stack.
My breath was gone, I couldn't yell, I couldn't even cry.
My brother's yelling for the folks, afraid I'm gonna die.
Then my father's face leans over me, his head blocks out the sun,
and he says if I don't start to breathe we're going to make a run
to that place where doctors work, called a hospital.
But the thought of doctors scared me into breathing after all

embi 5/18/11

~5~

The three of us shared kitchen chores , we'd rotate once a week.
Peeling turnips, spuds or carrots, sometimes we'd wash some leeks.
The piano stool would hold two kids standing near the sink.
The last kid's in the Frigidaire finding juice to drink.
When we finished cutting vegetables,
and our fingers made it through,
Mom would say which pot for which vegetables to use.
We had a stepstool for the stove, we could drop them in the pot,
while the pressure cooker in the back would bounce when it got hot.
The alchemy of cooking with it's magic took it's hold:
Our parents had their own techniques, one simple, one more bold.
My mother favored one pot meals, my dad would marinate.
His cast-iron skillet cleaned with salt, no soap touched what we ate.
Mom liked to use the Dutch-oven, but it got cleaned with soap.
When things got stuck, steel wool was used,
sometimes our only hope.

I'd been bitten by the cooking bug, my folks both showed me how,
a simple meal or work of art, stays with me even now.
Horsemeat was our main protein, stamped USDA blue.
The meat was leaner, slightly sweet, without the marbled glue.
The marinade my father made: red wine, bay leaf, fresh thyme,
with diced red onions, olive oil, fresh garlic and some lime
or lemon zest then some salt and black pepper,
then in the icebox overnight; the meat for next supper.
The odors from that marinade still stir a memory,
remembering work done as kids brings back my family.

embi 5/20/11

~6~

When I was little my dress code was a T-shirt nothing else.
Why this was I've no idea: no time to dress myself?
In a rush to get somewhere, discover a new game?
Cruising the house I hear Mom calling out my name.
I run into the kitchen, where the stool up to the stove
is still in place, inviting me, another place to rove.
My mom is at the kitchen sink, I climb up on the stool.
She's got apples waiting for the core and peeling tool.
Our stove was all electric, the manufacturer G.E.;
if you turned a burner on, it got red, so you could see.
It was when you turned the burner off, accidents occurred.
I turned to watch my mom then sat, on the front burner.
It wasn't red, must not be hot, but it just had been turned off.
The sizzle first and then the smell I tried to climb back off.
I'm yelling now, mom's holding me, my butt is almost done;
she peels me off and carries me to first aid on the run.
She finds a salve, crying with me, she's trying not to smile,
cause on my butt, I'm gonna have a bulls-eye for a while.

embi 5/2/11

~7~

One morning on a Sunday I went into the garage,
to get some spuds for breakfast, not be scared of a mirage
or ghost or boogey-man or whatever else he was.
The family car was parked indoors; it had a passenger.
I ran inside, a little freaked at how this might occur.
My mom came running from the front, my yelling upset her
enough so that my dad came in with soap on half his face.
By then the whole family's there, waiting just in case,
peering out the kitchen door staring at the place
where in the back seat of the car a hobo takes up space.
My father opens the car door, the odor was intense,
he asks the guy if he needs help, no shadow of pretense.
The hobo looks a little dazed, we're all waiting in suspense;
His apology's so quiet that we almost couldn't hear:
He'd drunk too much the night before and it wasn't only beer.
He was seeking shelter from the cold, that's what brought him here.
His story over breakfast seemed to make our parents sad.
I understood enough to know that times for him were bad.
He'd lost his job, his home, his wife, his world must have gone mad.
He left us wearing cleaner clothes, smelling better than he had.
And that night when I climbed into bed,
I thanked my mom and dad.

embi 5/27/11

~8~

A critical possession when you're of a certain age:
the skate key, it was sacred, it helped to set the stage.
Without it there was no way for the skate to stay in place,
and if a skate came off when racing, it's not just losing face;
the sidewalk tore your knees as well, it's hunger never died.
The tennie was no good for skates, we know, because we tried.
The grip in front that used the key would squash the tennis shoe.
At first we thought that a strong a grip was what we had to do.
But really what was missing was a shoe that had a sole.
My dress shoes were the perfect fit, tight grips, straps on, lets roll!!
Only, as I cross the living room, mom's standing at the door,
reminding once again that this is still a hardwood floor.
"No skates allowed inside the house," and
"What's with your dress shoes?"
I was busted, caught red-handed, no need to look for clues.
"Aww, Mom," I said, "I'll take good care,
we're just skating down the block."
"You leave the house with those shoes on,
the front door will be locked."
So much for thoughts of freedom, flying down the concrete walk;
first the skates and then the shoes, I'm too depressed to talk.
I'm certain she can't understand the need for the right tool.
Instead, she says, "We'll find you shoes at Goodwill after school."

embi 5/30/11

Pop's Whistle

My dad had a whistle that could fracture armored plate.
It could be an emergency or he'd simply be irate.
But when he blew, us kids all knew to get home yesterday,
not knowing, but afraid of, what he might have to say.

How he made that sound is still a mystery to me:
thumb and finger circled, then the mouth, that much I'd see.
What happened to the tongue and lips I haven't got a clue
but when we heard the shattered air, we all knew what to do.

Sometimes it was a simple thing like getting home too late
or dishes in the sink when we hadn't washed the plates.
Usually it meant that we had stuff we'd left undone --
Mom would start but Dad would stop, and bring us on the run.

The whistle also called our dog, Skitsi was her name,
short for schizophrenic, cause she had so many games.
A border collie, sometimes way too smart for her own good;
our yard was big but not enough, so she roamed the neighborhood.

Not coming home, sometimes just late,
Dad's whistle cracked the air.
When she came running, we'd all laugh, just glad to have her there.
Our neighborhood had cross streets that were hard to see around --
a car too fast, a dog on run, her body's what was found.

There was a second whistle, more melodic, gentle, kind.
That also called us, free of fear of trouble we might find.
My dad's dad played organ for a moving cinema.
He'd play that theme to tell his kids "go home and help your mom".

So two generations later we still used that melody,
like in the store our mom could tell us where she's gonna be.
Of all us whistlers, Dad's was best, whichever one he used.
For me it seemed the system worked, I never felt abused.

Fresh milk was part of our routine, it happened twice a week,
delivered by a happy guy who took the time to speak
a quick "hello", "good morning kid" or maybe just a wave:
four quarts of milk, the cream on top for butter we would save.

One morning's calm was shattered by a crash out in the street.
I ran up to the corner where I could see the driver's feet.
He'd been knocked out from the milk truck
by a car gone way too fast.
The street ran white with streaks of red,
they said both drivers "passed".

That corner held a sycamore; the tree forked left and right;
one side had a crow's-nest that gave righteous oversight;
the tree stood in the parkway on the street side of the walk,
so public use came naturally despite the neighbor's talk.

I'd sit up there for hours it seemed, my pirate ship at sea,
swaying back and forth enough to launch me bodily
across the space between the forks and catch the other branch,
then climb back down and up again to take another chance.

The father in the house that sat behind a picket fence
came out and told me to get down, somehow he took offence.
One day he came up after me, intent to bring me down.
I started swaying back and forth; his curse broke from his frown.

Angrily he came on up, grabbing for my foot.
I cast my self over his head, my landing was well put.
I shimmied down and hit the ground running, scared but glad.
I'd left Mr. Matheson up a tree and mad.

I remember breakfast time, we'd practice IPA,
an international alphabet my dad used for the play
of spoken words phonetically -- an easier way to spell.
Pencils near our oatmeal was one way that we could tell.

Lessons were available at home not just at school,
though neither parent gave out homework as a rule.
As teachers they both felt that the classroom was the space
for learning how to learn, so it can happen anyplace.

embi 11/03/13

Mom's Model A

Mom drove a Ford, a model A coupe that had to be thirty years old.
My kid brother and I would ride in the trunk,
the lid held up with a stick.
We got the stick from an old army cot;
we were both kinda proud of our trick.
We'd wave at the cars following us, loving the wind, and the cold.

Our rides in the trunk were mostly back roads,
less cars to notice our sport.
One favorite game was to bounce on the bumper,
springing the car up and down.
One day I decided to climb up to the front
where Mom met me with a frown.
Unspoken agreements had us stay in the trunk,
but that leaves no thrill to report.

On the way back home from the grocery store,
I was testing the bumper for bounce.
Then I looked down, saw the road rushing by and
wondered what it'd feel like
if I barely touched my foot on the ground.
Would my tennis shoe fly like a kite?
The road grabbed my foot, the other one too and
started right in with it's trounce.

My desperate grab of the bumpers' top rail
kept me from hitting the road.
My feet tried to run, my kid brother laughed;
he thought I was just having fun.
I couldn't keep up so my knees hit the road,
then my toes when attempting to run.
I knew to let go would hurt even more,
so my fear let my body be towed.

The car behind had a monstrous chrome grill and
started in honking his horn.
I'm sure all he wanted was for mom to pull over,
instead what she did was speed up.
While Mom tried to hurry out of the way,
the grinning grill waited to sup.
But the bounces in air just weren't long enough
to save my knees being torn.

When we rounded the corner the centrifugal force
almost pulled us apart.
How I held on I'll just never know,
since one of my hands twisted free.
Trying to grip, we pulled up to the house,
now my kid brother's staring at me.
Mom opens her door and walks back to the trunk
where the look on her face breaks my heart.

Shredded bare knees, torn shoes and toe tops
and a paralyzed grip on the car
were enough for my mom to cry out a note
I'd never heard, ever, before.
Prying my hand from the rear bumper strip,
Mom knows just to touch is too sore.
My father and mother get me into the bath,
while Mom hopes there won't be a scar.

Warm water turned pink and plain Epsom salts;
like a struck tuning fork I vibrate.
Mom cleans out the tears of gravel and tar
softly singing a song we both know.
Sitting on the commode, swinging both legs too fast,
my brother has no place to go.
While my sister stands still at the door to the hall
like a blond fairy guard at the gate.

My father checks in and looks at us all
and asks if we're having a wake.
Mom lifts up her head and looks back at him,
you can tell that she's already cried.
Mom laughs at Dad and turns back to me,
"You know you could of easily died?"
I heard what she said, so did everyone else
and I saw they were there for my sake.

embi 1/2/14

Grandpa Tarts

The gates to my grandfather's garden
all closed without help from the guest.
The magic was sash weights from windows
discarded and left with the rest
of the piles of recycled buildings.
I could stand in the gateway and wait,
till the swing of the gate found me standing,
wondering if I was late.
I told my grandpa I'd help him
in the garden with some of the weeds.
But help from a 7- or 8-year-old
doesn't fit, exactly, his needs.
Still, his smile diminishes caution,
letting wonder loose on the run.
I stare at the tipis of string beans,
and sunflowers catching the sun.
The garden has order that's simple;
the boxes are reached from both sides,
you can see down the lanes to the workshop,
where rakes, hoes and trowels abide.
My job is to pull weeds for grandpa,
but weeds in his garden are few.
Catching bugs might be good for the garden,
something that's more fun to do.
I don't know he's standing behind me,
while the beetle's not liking my game.
The sun off his glasses streaks past me,
and he asks, "Does your friend have a name?
Let's go pick some turnips and carrots,
and some beets to round out the roast."
Leg of a lamb from a farm up the back road,
for the dinner I liked the most.

The greens from the beets and the turnips
with garlic, onions and ham
go perfect with johnnycake pieces;
for this dinner, not walking, I ran.
So the play in the garden was grounded
in green beans and corn I could pick.
Pale green helmets of cabbage sit waiting,
while the dog from next door leaves his trick.

My grandfathers' nickname was Foxy,
everyone called him by that.
Too smart by most people's standards,
he rarely revealed where he's at.
Others did most of the talking,
he gathered while just standing still.
His chuckles, too few but engaging,
left others the spaces to fill.
Gophers were one of the problems
grandpa dealt with most every day.
He had traps on chains with a long stake
so the gopher couldn't drag it away.
The cats and the traps were the main guard,
though the shovel exposed one or two.
While the cats brought their trophies to show off,
for grandpa it's just what you do.
At the end of a hose a propeller
gave a fourth of the garden its' rain.
Each quarter of earth had a station,
one corner's was right in the lane.
Mud puddles a target for stomping,
would cause some concern for our mom.
Shoes carried the dirt through the household,
each one a truck of small bombs.

The squash blossom flowers we'd harvest,
egg batter, bread crumbs, and then fried.
A bounty of blessings, this garden,
since the neighborhood too was supplied.
Time with grandpa was sparse and infrequent,
a pleasure I'd welcome again.
His wisdom was subtle and tricky;
I'd learn but I didn't know when.
The house was full of the women,
two aunts, my mom and grandma,
two older cousins, both female,
left my brother and me with grandpa.

So us "men" were outside in the garden,
harvesting what's ripe for our meals,
while songs could be heard from the household,
I'm pleased by the comfort I'd feel.
My grandfather's hat mocked a "trilby",
a medium brim capped his head.
His bandana, kept in his back pocket,
I remember the color was red.
He'd use it for sweat or his glasses,
pausing to stare into space,
then to earth and the dirt in the garden.
There was never enough of this place!

embi 9/11/13

Butano Creek

(with family and friends)

She runs with the boys,
        sure, swift, slight and blond.
While I challenged, teased
        and bragged about who
would be first off the cliff
        into the pool at the bottom
of the falls, she had already
        launched herself into space.
Our mouths open and
        our egos beyond repair,
we were left with false
        bravado and "we planned
it that way". Roger and I
        followed my sister, with
the twins and my kid brother,
        coming after, hoping they
won't land on our heads.

At the cost of a few
        skinned knees, elbows
and torn fingernails,
        our sport consisted of
climbing the jagged,
        wet, side of the falls
in order to jump into
        the head of the falls
and have it knock us
        back into the pool
while trying to reach
        the bottom, which

did occur, time to time.
          She would bring up
a handful of silt as
          proof of reaching
the bottom of the pool.

The hike up to the falls
          included a walk on the edge
of the creek, usually
          wading past woods, meadows
and occasional summer
          homes. The creek held
brown and speckled trout
          as well as steelhead. Roger
was a serious fisherman
          and we would look for
fishing holes on the way
          up to the falls. Displaying
a patience I didn't know
          I had, Roger taught me
the stillness necessary
          to allow the fish to trust
our lures. Betrayed by
          mans' hunger and ingenuity,
they became a delightful
          dinner.

Sometimes an adult
          would make a suggestion/
request, sending us on
          a mission with bacon
and string. Our "job"
          was to catch as many
crawfish as we could.
          Of course there was the

occasional frog, lizard or
           inchworm while waiting
for the bacon, tied and sitting
           on the bottom of the creek,
gathering a convention of
           crawdads, to be slowly and
gently elevated to within
           reach of our nets. Sis didn't
appear to be bothered by
           the twins' attempt to scare
her with members of
           our catch. Half a century
later, I'm still in awe of
           the creek's generosity.

embi 4/4/14

Fall and Leaving

The leaves of the elm tree are leaving.
The steel gurney stands sentinel below.
Red and black, black and red are the colors
announcing the neighborhood show.

Bathrobes and curlers and T-shirts,
slippers and flip flops, some shoes.
Fashion has taken a backseat,
while the sidewalk broadcasts the news.

Portuguese cookies she crafted.
The kids couldn't wait til they're done.
Though the parents might balk at the sweet treats,
even they have been known to have one (or two).

She had a small garden with flowers,
and vegetables used in her meals.
Her flavors were different than our house --
just that alone had appeal.

When she spoke you could hear the old country,
and she sang songs she'd learned as a child.
If you sat she might tell you a story,
though at times they might sound a bit wild.

Her gift was the mystery of foreign,
her accent a cadence outside,
not of our day-to-day patter,
lost now on the night that she died.

Our vigil in silence is pensive.
Is there family to handle affairs?
Her strays will need new homes come morning.
I'm hoping the neighborhood cares.

My mom's hand is warm and a comfort.
She's quiet and sad, I can tell.
I'll miss the stories and singing,
and the cookies' most magical smell.

The leaves of the elm tree are leaving,
and Sophia is gone with the fall.
The colors she loved are returning;
now her goodness is ours to recall.

embi 9/9/11

LIFE SENTENCE

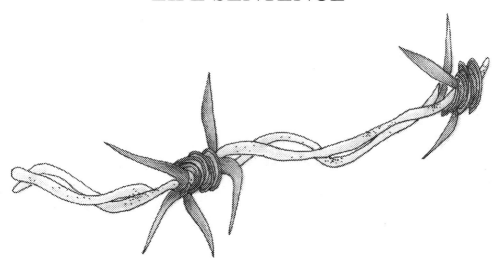

Time Thief

The other day the doctor's office held the usual feng shui.
The past three months were conversations all about the search,
so when I asked if he had found what the tests would show me,
he couldn't tell by looking that he'd knocked me off my perch.

I know I've done some crazy stuff; it's a wonder I'm still here,
but from left field, the cool blue moon, or a month of Sundays still
did not explain a visit that the ugly truth made clear:
that time is precious only if there's not enough to fill.

Up til then the notion was the end was still abstract,
not bracketed by terminal -- free time a sound belief .
Today I have to tell myself to try to not lose track
of those who love and share my life and offer some relief.

I thought of time as mine, to do with as I please.
I realize now that time's on loan to steward with respect,
that moving on includes the grace of giving others ease
without the burden common to the time spent on regrets.

embi 3/20/12

Guess Who's Come for Dinner

I have an uninvited guest, who doesn't want to leave but
I think I know what's best, so my kin won't have to grieve.
While his appetite is viscous regardless of the host,
to him it's most delicious when the host becomes a ghost.

Providing for his exile is not a simple task,
but to go that extra mile is what I have to ask
of myself and family, both extended and close friends,
to deal with this anomaly before we reach the end.

His occupation devastates the space he uses up,
including outside landscapes or inside where he sups.
We've joined the bloody battle, my friends, my wife and I,
though I can't but feel like cattle while the AMA tells lies.

We've found successful protocols from doctors who have won;
not just any port of call, you can see the work they've done.
Hospitals and pharmacies and insurance companies --
each one supports a fallacy meant to maintain the disease.

I must admit this bag of skin I wear that holds this soup
is frightening when the roommate's in and forces me to stoop.
If you're watchful for a minute you can see the muscles twitch,
you'd think a snake was in it, it can almost make you itch.

Mainstream medicine won't tell you where to find a cure.
If it involves nutrition, the line becomes obscure.
If it involves a growth hormone, outside the standard call,
they won't bother with the telephone, they'll send a paper wall.

The protocol for this disease is FDA approved,
administered as if to please those whom it most behooves;
not the patients, they just die, but the drug's sold anyway --
what good it does is half a lie, "good question" as they say.

The side effects belie the good, argues quality of life.
Still alive! as if that would be enough amongst the strife
of lost control, inch by inch, someone else to wipe my ass,
food by tube, it's a cinch, a lung pump in a glass?

Do we become so desperate that to keep the mind alive,
we rent a respirator so just the brain survives?
What's hard for me to understand is the politics of death: if
to argue, challenge, take a stand and fight the loss of ethics
is too much for the average guy, then who takes up the fight?
Doctrines used without a why are wearing blindfolds in the night.

embi 4/17/12

Resurrection (for June)

Oblivion, colorless
cold oblivion,
frigid molasses movement
against time
as solid as adobe
in winter. No
hope. What is hope?
Darkness answers
with darkness.

Time not time,
space not space.
Waiting,
what's waiting?
Who's waiting?
She's waiting!
He: he is; he is he,
awake. Is he?
Is is?

A gold coin,
a distant moon,
a sun of face:
her face, a place!
A place towards:
a direction!
Up! Up against
the tar, the tar of
oblivion.

A light, a sacred
light, her face,
a pulse, beyond reach,
a glimmer. Jello
movement, awareness
drugged, the light,
gone. Again
the void holds
the swimmer.

The tunnel
becomes
a tunnel when
light becomes.
The light, her face,
the swimming crawl
to reach the light,
the moon,
her face,
her.

embi 11/12/13

24/7/365

(a day in the life)

Will I ever sleep in my bed again?
Will I ever wake with my wife?
Will my hands stop their curling into bird claws,
is there a chance for a near normal life?

I ask these questions in fear and in hope,
while unwanted changes arrive.
My breath is run by a breathing machine.
Is a wall plug what keeps me alive?

I think of my dog and my wife home alone
and our deck where we'd sit in the sun.
She'd have wine I'd have juice with the sun going down
in our loveseat, just swinging for fun.

The simple things that are missing right now
like, to stand alone and not fall,
or not using two hands while brushing my teeth,
or unzipping my fly at the call.

I want a sunburn on my back and my butt
and to be able to sleep on my side.
This hospital bed and gravity both,
want to help take my soul for a ride.

This hose in my throat rides down my chest
where it takes a right turn at my waist.
Every thing that I do has to remember this,
or I pay if I'm moving in haste.

My wheelchair's OK but the brakes are in back
and coming and going gets tough.
Especially since I have to call for support
so my oxygen tank has enough.

A baby's first breath is a true miracle,
young lungs free to grab the new air;
but without this machine my lungs might collapse
since all by myself is so rare.

We're working to strengthen my lungs with my walks;
for my arms, adding pushups as well.
All this time this malaise never stops in it's work,
so at times I gain insights to hell.

To get up out of bed and just cross the room
without the hose and the chair
is a dream and a wish every minute I breathe
and I know, yes, life sometime's not fair.

A walk up my road with my dog on a leash
toward my home I built with my friends,
past tall Redwood stands and Bay Laurel groves,
the dog checking each fern in the glen.

A memory now, that I cherish each time
I think of the way I walk now,
the walker, the wheelchair, the vent on five wheels:
sorta feels like I'm pushing a plow.

The work that I do is called therapy,
designed to get better; get well!
Progress is a theory that proves true sometimes,
but at others, seems no one can tell.

At times I get caught in my thoughts of my work
left undone at my home on the ridge,
knowing now that I'm not the one for the job;
so failure becomes one more bridge.

Fixing things was a pleasure I got, when it worked,
and our home had many such chores.
Raingutters, deck trim, roof leaks and new paint
Just a few and of course there are more.

All this falls to my wife who already works
more hours than God gave a week.
So I reach out to friends who are willing enough,
but where's the time that gets spent as we speak.

My room has a door to a courtyard outside
made of glass that allows the wheelchair
passage enough for escape to outdoors.
How I treasure the gift of fresh air!

embi 11/12/13

Baby Hands

I now have the hands of a baby:
slight grip, unsure and wanting,
reaching to hold, hoping to grasp
while exploring the new limitations.

The left hand has to hold the right
hand just to reach the spoon left in
the coffee cup, to stir the French
Roast fine grind into suspension.

The suspense of this disease is which
part will begin to declare its inability
to perform its completely taken for
granted, natural god given, ability.

The forefinger of my left hand just
hangs, unable to lift to point or push
my glasses back up my nose. I use my
thumb. Raising my arm has become

a challenge. Sometimes I have to
ask for help. When no one is present,
I ask for patience, which is also, some
times, not present. Learning GRACE

in the face of daily, minute by minute,
failure is a Karmic duty I did not
anticipate. Learning, fortunately,
continues like it or not. The boot

I wear, eight-to-twelve twice a day,
is helping to keep my left foot from
becoming like my hands; curled and
confused, like a curious new baby's.

embi 3/2/14

Fetus

Alone in the courtyard
head, neck, back
and hands curled
as if rounding
himself against
the onslaught
of nerves
under attack.

The wheels of his chair
echo the curve
of his body,
reminding me
of Kokopeli,
whose contagious
misbehavior mimics
the bacteria.

One foot to push, one foot
to drag, gnarled
hands to wheel
to unopened
doors. Club
hands pull
to open; we watch
from our beds

through glass doors
also closed. Speech
altered by broken
motor nerves,
too proud to
ask for help,
he remains
alone in the courtyard.

embi 11/19/13

Mistress of The Dance

Sometimes it seems that death is losing patience.
Sometimes her indifference gives me chills,
not unlike a girlfriend wanting her own space,
still the knowing without dying makes me ill.

I know she's been here since I found my first breath,
but like a sibling that is easily ignored,
her presence in the background is never quite forgotten
until her dance steps finally take me off the floor.

For some her presence offers up a simple peace,
for others she's a terror beyond words.
For me my fear's about the work I've left undone,
thinking this current vessel could's absurd.

To think that keeping death at bay is arrogance
I recognize as foolish, even humorous.
I've witnessed many fantasies of stalling death
from late night campfires to movies; it's in all of us.

As a partner in this dance of life I recognize
now, how fragile is the very choreography
that slows or tries at least to minimize
the moment when my partner's finally done with me.

Her presence has been always, but my noticing
is more frequent since I walk these hopeless halls
and see the litter of the disrepaired and broken down
left still staring at these yellowed ivory walls.

I'm a transient member of this frail community,
committed to escaping with my soul intact.
But the moments when my partner hovers over me
make the days seem like I'm starting to lose track.

I've started naming holes and cracks worn in the floor,
observed on walks I labor through five days a week.
Hanging from my walker I greet every one.
She laughs because I can't get them to speak.

A tracheotomy has helped to make my roommate mute,
when we visit, he writes I talk, we get along,
and I notice my dance partner's fairweatherness
since the whore of death will dance to every song.

embi 2/12/14 & 3/21/14

Elderberries

Too soon we are elders.
When did that occur?
I see a picture of my sister
holding my granddaughter,
one glowing, one fading,
both captured in time.

In the gym, in the mirror,
sometimes I see myself
and am startled, again.
In my mind's eye there
is no wheelchair, no
trachea hose to the ventilator.

My Exercycle to nowhere
is peddling me to Carmel
by the sea, in my dream.
My double tiered walker
is my motorcycle down
the hallways to the hi-ways.

Most visitors are polite,
positive, supportive and
encouraging. Some are
more candid, perhaps
more realistic. None are
seeking enlightenment.

But isn't that what elders
are for? Wisdom in a
wheelchair? I suppose
anything is possible. How
"to be of use", to contribute,
from here, with what's left?

embi 2/27/14

Wail Watching

I've heard the music
of a whale singing
to it's pod, the carols
of the coyotes'
moonlight ensemble
and the crickets'
banjo staccato,
all sharing their part
of our mother's
symphony with
the blues of a barn owl
alone in the night, and
the jazz riff of a mockingbird,
contrapuntal to it's mate's,
with the early morning's
minor etude by the
ring neck doves
orchestrating the gift
of sound held dear
but
the high pitched peal
of fear,
the saw-edged strings
of fury,
the percussive shatter
of pain,
the brass horn howl
of rage
the amplified echo
of hopelessness
all compose
the other
side of that same
symphony.

Each day I listen
for music
but what happens
in these halls
hurts to hear.
So I listen outside
of the everyday,
where my memory
and imagination
gift those miracles
I heard at home.

embi 2/20/14

Terminal Gifting

My visits to the terminals -
family, friends and relations -
were never acutely aware of
the microseconds, the moments,
the minutes, the hours
day and night, abandoned,
awake, afraid and alone.

The need, nay, the craving for
respect, affection, and dignity
are all sublimated by "duty"
and the ministrations of the
DOCTOR'S ORDERS. Having
been a more conventional
statistic, I can say that this
category sucks!!!

Being ignored, talked over,
overlooked and filled with
politely smiled empty
promises, provides this
living mausoleum with the
atmosphere of a behind
the counter butcher shop
rearranging the carcasses.

Being left naked while
a parade of aides files through,
to stop and discuss their
needs for other patients,
as well as the daily gossip,
has stripped away any
pretense of recognition
as a human being.

Being a slab of meat,
anointed three times
a day with soap and water,
meets the coded requirements
of the county and state
while sorely missing
"human contact" but is
still considered humane.

If it weren't for the infrequent
ANGELS who visit as workers,
family and friends, "hell"
would be a polite description
and "purgatory" a visit to a
country club. And yes, I know
it can always get worse!
It has and does, just not
yet spoken.

What I've come to regret
was my continued neglect
of the human beings left
to their own devices when
my discomfort or convenience
would not allow the "grace"
necessary for the other
person's solace and comfort.

Insight becomes a burden
when guilt invades our space.
"Being" with others
and their anguish and
uncertainty requires a
personal harmony I
only see when LOVE
is truly present.

I ask forgiveness for my
trespasses over and through
my own heart, let alone,
all the others I've managed
to dent, crumple, damage,
crush, void, spindle, harm
or hurt. I'm also aware of
too little, too late.

embi 4/11/14

Peace

I pray for peace;
even as I write
I look
for that place
apart,
where the settling
of the soul
resounds.

The mantle
of the whole
enfolds and cradles
me and mine
in certainty
and calm
with the flow of
the golden river.

Floating amongst
the souls
of the blessed,
I see invitation
and sanctuary.
Inspired reason
alone, enough
for harbor.

Flowing on
and in
I lay down
and let go
my fears
and discomforts,
disintegrating self
in the current.

Oscillating rings
of sound vibrate
my cells,
like the echo of
bells in the canyons
of the city,
sharing me
with the river.

My sound is
lifted and sent
to freedom beyond
bodies and walls,
garnering purpose
and place in
the ether
of space.

I am gathering
my will to live
on with the now
in light and grace
flowing within
and without
a final
resting place.

embi 1/18/14

MUSINGS & MEANDERINGS

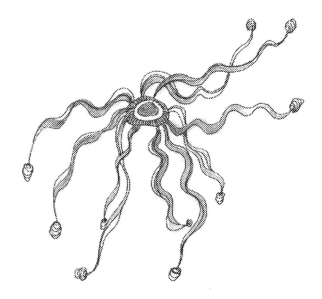

Colonary Insights

Mutton Geoff and Rosemarie
out lambing from the chops,
hiding out with Olivia
who drives a lemon when she shops.
Sir Rathbone* and his partner Spud
sat bacon in the sun,
as if their skillets had them
lard it over everyone.
If things aren't claret nough by now,
no cheese comes with the whine.
Gourmand pretense more sage than I
says squash before you dine.**
Remember friends and family.
Just don't dessert them all.
Shed a tiramisu for a crème broulee
when it's Sauterne to take the call.
Remember fun and profiteroles
can help to make your day.
And any doppio can use
house coffee for au lait.

* Sir Basil Rathbone, Shakespearean actor, played Sherlock Holmes,
and the Sheriff of Nottingham with Errol Flynn
     ** "Wash before you dine!"
     *** doppio: double expresso

embi 4/29/10

Remembering

Does the savoring of the past recreate or create? Is the memory a
filtered amalgamation? Is the process of remembering about
realigning chemicals so as to build familiarity? Since the past is in the
past, what's a memory? My particular thoughts don't pose the past in
the past; some folks have even been known to state that the past is
never in the past. What I've noticed is that some of the memories
I've collected have a more poignant flavor/presence than others. My
wondering has me looking at whether or not I realized their
uniqueness at the time. We can always look back (an interesting
rearrangement of the meaning of looking) and flavor or spice up
some memory or other, but recognizing special moments, in the
moment, doesn't always happen. Having history as a reference is
much different than having history as a curse. I've been known to
use my memories as a form of self flagellation and I question
whether or not that was my intent. "Feeling bad," an expression that
populates our conversations, takes on different meanings when
using memory as the trigger. For example, I can recall mistakes I've
made where someone else has suffered and use that to beat myself
up (I should say down, those memories rarely generate up) or we
have physical conditions that provide real pain. In school I was
taught that the mind does not remember pain, for which I'm
extremely grateful. I can remember a lot of things but the pain of
pain isn't one of them and I wonder what part of that technique we
can learn or have learned when we filter our memories. I can
remember sitting under our lime tree with Pepper, our Dalmatian, in
the morning sunlight just breathing together not doing anything but
being together.

I can remember riding my motorcycle to work one morning and the wind was up and stirring the trees so as to cause them to lose their petals. On that day the trees I passed loosed pink, yellow and purple confetti into the air I was riding through. I get that back when I visit that memory but am I disqualified from the present when recollecting? I choose to believe that we make present our past, which includes it in the present.

embi 3/15/12

In The Light

I've got family waiting, good friends are there too,
wishing won't hurry my being with you.
When I hold you in reverence and stone gratitude,
Again I'm reminded how you feed my soul food.
I give thanks for the light in the halls of my heart.
You've given me reason to embrace a new start.
When the spirit is willing but the body is slow,
I can laugh and remember it's the way we all go.

Rejoice in the giving of the life that we hold,
and cherish the gift all our memories have told.
We share with each other our time on this earth,
knowing God is a mystery that begins with our birth.
Your light fills my chalice; it washes your word
in the delicate fabric of the song of a bird.

The music of water gives us life as we know it,
while the magic of stars births an awe when you show it.
When it's time to cross over and the passing is plain,
I pray my life's efforts have not been in vain.
I've heard good intentions pave the highway to hell,
and the stairway to heaven claims the climb will end well.
With no worries when leaving (especially if late)
I wonder what changes as I pause at the gate.

If the gatekeeper's Whoopi then I know I've arrived,
cause it means love's a promise that somehow survived.
Regrets are the curse of life's incompletions,
the fewer the better or so I've been told.
It'd be good if they faded like freckles and starlight
and left only wonder at being so old.
OLD, that's a good one, is it time or time spent?
Some live long and prosper, some can't pay the rent.

Could we, through our efforts to live through each day,
show wisdom as ageless so our children can play?
A child can be older than paint in a boat,
eating hopeless for dinner, leaving laughter remote.
Yet adult adolescence can be so out of place,
you wonder if God's made a joke of our race.
It's hard to be grateful when I look at the others
without simple choices; they're my family my brothers.

So I try to remember to share what I've got
and shorten the distance between the have and have not.
If I can lighten life's burdens with a poem or a song,
I'm grateful God chose to have me along.
The ride's still amazing from my point of view,
I've been lucky and blessed, all my thanks go with you.

embi 5/13/10

Earth Bound

If we walk in the shoes of our neighbors' old news,
there's a chance they might call you brother.
Righting the wrong is only part of the song;
the balance is up to each other.
Eye to eye sight can see both of you right,
even when "wrong" is the color.
Backing off your ideas, so you hear some of his,
might make your life brighter, not duller.

We get lost in the might when we all think we're right,
so original thoughts lose their standing.
But when questions are raised and the questioner's hazed,
popularity becomes more demanding.
If you're part of a mob whose intent is to rob
the right to pursue happiness
from those different than you, be they Muslim or Jew,
you've ignored you're the cause of the mess.
How many years and how many tears
and how many lives do we lose?
Mired in ancient techniques, it goes on as we speak
while we discard our duty to choose.

With consumers in debt, with a job that won't let
the taxpayers' head above water,
we're then offered the lies our leaders supply
to justify foreign soil slaughter.
Now the banks have all lied, decent reason has died
while indifference has grown out of greed.
Where does sanity stay, when does common sense say,
"That's enough, how much more do we bleed?!"
When our politics chase the petroleum base
with complete disregard for the planet,
then the balance is gone and the greedy have won
leaving our EarthShip with pirates to man it.

We know our system has flaws when the rich make the laws
and the meek shall inherit their graves.
If we can't change it now, we may never learn how,
while our children grow up to be slaves.
The earth was a place that gave birth to our race
but we're killing our mother instead.
Once we've plundered her core and left nothing more,
then the living will envy the dead.

embi 4/24/11

Time to Time

Do we come of age as youngsters,
like when our best friend leaves,
or the childhood crush collapses
in an angst we can't believe?

What if age and time are different
and wisdom just a spark,
that settles for an instant
but still leaves us in the dark.

When trusting circumstances is
a folly learned too late,
then we're for a moment wiser
with our answers out of date.

If we recognize distinctions
but don't bend to use the tool,
we waste an opportunity,
hoping not to look the fool.

I've noticed that acceptance
looks a lot like giving up,
but some battles aren't worth fighting;
like a storm in a tin cup.

As youngsters we're immortal;
to climb a mountain's fun
and the universe still offers
random choices on the run.

In our youth we're simply guessing
what "responsible" should mean
and end up learning wishes
can fall to might-have-beens.

So we make it through our childhood
unaware as young adults
that the passage never ends
and some failures have no fault.

When it's time to raise a family
and we're blessed with healthy kids,
do they go through what we went through,
do they do the things we did?

A "hope in hell" is plenty,
if they've learned enough to learn,
but too often our suggestions
helped to drive them to the burn.

I've no faith that there's an answer,
I just wish that it were so;
to save some grief through wisdom
rarely happens, as we know.

So that when our children find us,
often after their own stress,
that's the time we share our struggles,
to help sort out the mess.

If laughter's part of memory
while we seek enlightenment
and changes change and then change back,
then our passage paid the rent.

To recognize the river's flow
through each generation's child,
gives insight into history
being made, but not yet filed.

To know acceptance as our choice
and not a default mode,
leaves Buddha, Christ, and Mohammed
at peace, walking the same road.

embi 3/27/11

Home Again, Home Again

I can't help but
notice the noise
of silence.
It holds the sounds
of all things
but none
are heard,
only my
cerebral
echoes.

The overloud clarity
of sunlight
that warms the breeze
scattering old leaves
and new petals,
too early blooming,
while the muted
shade cools
that same
breeze.

The courtyard
setting of painted
concrete, peeling
its barn red skin,
butts against
dead orange
stucco walls
and sliding glass
doorways where
wheelchairs and
aides pass.

A row of houses,
backs to the tracks,
sat across the street
from my block
where my house
stood, four houses
from the corner.
My curiously
enlightened family
had room for dreams.

At night
in my upper bunk,
I would let
the rhythmic
clacking of
the trains and
their whistles
take me to
faraway and magical
places.

Today, when I hear
the growl of a
motorcycle
fading away,
it becomes my
midnight train,
taking me to faraway
and magical places.
I've always loved
that haunted
windborne
whistle.

embi 2/23/14

Beyond Repair?

She walks without regard for hell
or heaven.
Her soul's tripping over sidewalks
grey with helplessness.
The space above our clouds
becomes a dumping ground zero
left or right of stardust
falling backwards.

The circus left a trodden
field of emptiness,
the laughter lying
shattered in the grass.
The sun burst and bled itself
dry with humor
best left unspoken,
leaving silence crippled
with good ideas.

Everywhere the air
turned east
and felt like
saran-wrap,
smothering faith,
hope and charity
in a glass embrace.

Wolves sang
hunger songs
of children without
breakfast or
a pair of shoes
to advertise
the broken road
of early death
and salvation.

Glaciers melting
into our fears
of not enough,
help swell
the tides of
relentless greed,
laying bare
the breast of our
mother earth to
the carnivores
of commerce.

Against the moon
hour habit pulls
us out of harmony
with the present,
twisting the path
to the past like
barbed wire
around Tule Lake
and Manzanar.

Coastal waters
gleaming with
petroleum's sheen,
showcasing
a variety of
carcasses preserved
in fossil fuel,
left for our future
generations'
unnatural
playground.

Toxic cities
exploding into
the countryside
like molten lava
laying down a
carpet filled with
terminal disease,
disregarded
and denied in
gilded rhetoric,
surfing the surface
of pretense.

Cataclysmic offerings
grace our garden
of broken bounty
in protest of the
carnage crafted
out of wanton
disregard for
the spirit
of the blue sphere
circling a stellar gift
we still continue
to ignore.

embi 5/14/14

TRIBUTES

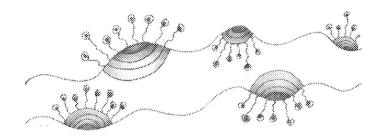

Bryar

Newborn purple, blue and wrinkled,
a hematoma for a hat.
To my eyes there wasn't anything
as magical as that.
His vocal protest: music to
the awestruck ears of dad.
Exhausted Mom, triumphant smiles,
in wonder still, at what we had.
I'd see him with his mom at rest,
content with plain and simple things,
and notice something pure and whole,
discovering the peace it brings.
I'd watch him figure out a game
he'd build in his own way,
then he'd laugh and spill the structure's walls,
the new already into play.
Content to share up to the point
when taking stops the play,
then restoring balance fearlessly
as if there is no other way.

He took the time to learn a craft
from scratch, just like the saying goes.
A cook, a chef, then food maestro:
the art of freedom, well won. It shows
in his work, his wife, his sons and friends.
He's teaching me a gentle grace,
through children of his own he lends
strength and wisdom equal space.
His gift to us is being here,
giving everyone an easy berth.
Reserved and poised, a ready ear,
from him we all can know our worth.

embi

Nova

Catching her around the waist,
letting go then giving chase.
Squeals and laughter, brooks and bells,
such joy and freedom; can you tell
she's my daughter?

Too fast, too soon, now she has friends.
Blind to my need to make amends:
her world's begun, mine nearly ends
without my daughter.

She brings her friends for overnight.
I see these children in new light;
a woman-child now in my sight.
Where goes my daughter?

Her wisdom overtakes the need
for global, local, family creed;
she gives back and takes the lead
and still my daughter.

A woman now, who fights to stay
free, to go her own way,
and begs the question: when can I play
with my granddaughter?

embi 4/5/10

Ethan

(Grandson)

Do we choose indentured servitude so our children have a voice?
Is going to work eight days a week really our only choice?
To bring a child into this world then live your life for him,
making sure the choice you made wasn't just a whim.
The second son was born with pain that showed with every cry;
that agony they faced each day without the what or why.
With different doctors chasing pain, looking for a cure,
but the first and second probables left no one really sure.
The need was clear, the answer not, until they found the holes.
But the remedy would take some time and minutes tried their souls.
When finally they had made him whole, his language had begun.
He'd learned requesting through his pain; help, always on the run.
These days his older brother helps (patience beyond belief)
while mom and dad are busy finding ways to lend relief.
His special day is May the Fifth, notable worldwide.
Could that have special meaning or simply coincide?
Birthdays frequently omit the first home of the child;
the mom who carried him til birth gets the backseat for a while.
Just long enough to view the chaos young ones all call fun,
then salvage order til next time, the work is never done.
It helps to notice gratitude despite exhaustion's weight.
The sacrifice for happiness is happiness in state.
All in all, a gift, the boy, to those of us who care.
Knowing all that he's been through,
we're just grateful that he's there.

embi 5/5/10

The Art of Paul

A maple leaf suspended in
the headlights of my car,
Garfunkel and Simon sharing
silence while the stars
reflect time and space,
we're believing that we are
both precious and distinct.

I've yet to understand
the aching in my heart
when I think of friends who've passed,
leaving memories as part
of moving on, and living life
as if we're works of art
about to become extinct.

Fall and falling leaves announce
the change that winter brings,
leaving desolate and naked
trees where the last leaves cling
as if holding on will change results
like growing pairs of wings
while standing on the brink.

If angels choose to gather,
does believing let them in?
Are we and they as much a part
of living with our sins?
If all of space can gather
on the head of one small pin,
maybe life is just a blink.

Still part of me is missing from
the time and space we rent,
when I find myself remembering
moments squandered, lost or spent,
just wishing I could do again.
My hindsight won't relent,
I guess it costs me just to think.

What brings about this rush of tears
while sitting at the wheel?
Are sights and smells and sounds enough
to alter how we feel?
When your friends become your family,
is that part of the deal?
Maybe that's the missing link.

Sometimes a lost connection
need not be lost at all. Since
remembering rebuilds the myth
from pieces we recall,
like leaves of autumn in the wind
the grace is in the fall,
leaving winter one last drink.

embi 12/5/10

Good Jobs

1955-2011

He was only fifty six, yet his work has changed the world.
My only way of knowing him was filtered through my son.
He had a wife and children and a home with in-house chef,
while his eating habits challenged him and almost everyone.

Recipes were copied, some were borrowed, some just bought,
others were experiments brought home from other parts.
His tastes, somewhat eclectic, maybe "strange" a better word
since his travels showed him kitchens making different works of art.

Food for him was held as fuel, sometimes social played a part,
but finding what was useful didn't always taste that good,
so my son would have to reconstruct from what worked in the past
and bring in new ingredients with techniques he understood.

To make it right sometimes meant bringing water from Japan,
or spending time in a kitchen where English has no voice,
or a kitchen up in Napa where food building is an art
that employs hi-tech techniques -- a very different choice.

Imagine that the mind that has his chef explore the world
has visions for the rest of us that we can't comprehend,
yet changed our day in such a way that makes life magical
by building all of us a tool that connects and heals and mends.

His technology has given us connections round the world,
we can see and hear and speak ourselves in the language of the host.
We can even see our world up close or from space like astronauts.
Regardless of your point of view, his tools become his ghost.

From hip-pockets of designer jeans to shelves on bedroom walls,
his genius has helped alter us in ways we still don't know.
Our children speak a language in a text that's alien,
already universal in most countries on the go.

John Lennon said the Beatles were more popular than Christ.
For a moment that was true but so what, unless we
can use the music of the world to bridge the different faiths.
With the iPhone now there is a chance to alter history.

Steve Jobs has touched the whole world with ways to interact:
to know the size and weight of time in Mozambique and Rome,
and grasp the notion of the ocean on this planet earth,
to hear and see and feel the wars near or far from home.

Communication is a start, that much he's given us.
An example is the folks out marching in the streets,
their cell phones linked to marchers 3000 miles away,
all united in a cause, though they may never meet.

I'm grateful for conveniences that save me time and grief,
like microchips that open doors and tell my stove to stop.
I even find myself in stores, my cell against my ear,
hearing my wife calling me while we're still in the same shop.

What we're calling hi-tech now was science fiction then.
When Dick Tracy wore wrist TVs and rockets flew to Mars.
The world is changed; we're smaller now,
we know more than we need.
Steve's given us some basic tools, our next stop is the stars.

embi 10/10/11

Bernie

(the passing of a friend, engineer and inventor)

He didn't ask me, he didn't say goodbye.
He was one of us, he wasn't just some guy.
His leaving was so sudden --
yes, we knew that it was time,
but we all weren't really ready for our friend to die.

We all know that it's coming, and sooo not ready when it's here.
Yesterday was different, we knew you still were near.
Today the body's empty;
there's a space without your voice,
and left pondering your passage are those that held you dear.

You were well respected, some even called you wise.
You were our tribal Solomon, if only to us guys.
Cantankerous and testy?
Sure, at times, just like us all.
But hugs and laughter contradict the love you can't disguise.

Your woman's ultra special; she helped to hold the space,
by making room for all of us while holding us in place.
Inside the home, a spectacle
with magic spoken there.
Her love for you was obvious, you could see it on her face.

Your departure left a vacancy we can't fix or fill.
Not just you, your shadow's gone, your sleeping chair is still.
We'll miss you, Bernie Gerber,
you're a friend held in our thoughts.
We're holding that you're better now, no need for all those pills.

As long as we're alive, you're in our minds and hearts.
Your children and your grandchildren all carry different parts.
Your genius is their future;
your insight is a gift.
You've shown us that your good ideas were not just works of art.

embi 7/14/11

Lyrrin

(Granddaughter)

I like
hanging out
on the corners
of your mouth.
Laughter,
like a cradle
holding
innocence,
spills itself
into mischief.

Bending lines
drawn
in the sands
of reason,
while testing,
every moment
you're
awake.

Delight
captured
in the honey
of your giggle
lets me give
up holding up
my so-called
grand design.

The privilege of
your presence
grants a miracle
co-opted by
your very own
community
made of angels,
sunlight, tears
and laughing
teddy bears.

Your reach
is so much
farther than
what we know
or even what
we're ready for.
I wonder at your
wonder and your
bright inquiry
into everything!

All your mothers
make our world
accessible by
gifting us the
chronicles of your
evolution. Their
embrace embraces
all of us. I'm
grateful we are
in our lives.

embi 5/16/14

BITS & PIECES OF ME AND NATURE

Cloud Ships

Where do the clouds go
day after day,
floating like ships on
a celestial bay?

They come and they go
and they sometimes leave rain;
yet each one is different
and won't come again.

Marshmellow pillows
for giants to sleep,
or smoke turned to cream puffs
for children to eat.

How often I've wondered
just how far from home,
I'd be were I climbing
those mountains of foam.

embi 8/13/62

Morning Winds

New leaves dance on
branches moved
by breezes chased
from the bay,
up the gulch and
over the ridge.
Does the wind
have as much
fun as I
imagine?
Do grasses love
the wind's caress?
Do trees hear
the wind's whisper?
Does the arbor feel
the buffet and
the embrace?
To cherish something
simple is both
surprising and delightful.

Greens riot against
high blue ether, neither
winning nor losing,
both clean,
clear and comforting
as if by intention.
My eyes see
the day wonder
full. Notes of metal
and wood splash
into my hungry ears,
chiming the wind's
arrival.
Remembering
paper and string,
kites and kids,
racing and chasing
the wind.

embi 4/27/11

Water for Hummingbirds

The point,
submerged in the fall's cascade
while suspended in mid-air
on invisible wings,
allows thirst a respite.

Bullets with wings
visit the ceramic waterfall
on their way
to flowered nectar.
Leaving so swift, the thought --
did I see what I saw?

Magic! It is magic
to appear and disappear
in a blink.
A short life of sips
of water and flower and
flower and water.

Almost here,
an iridescent dart,
a taste, a sip then gone.
Do they sleep at night?
Do they dream,
of other birds, fatter flowers,
bigger falls?

Window,
stunned, in my palm:
the pulse more rapid than I
can measure, while
its tiny claws find and hold
my finger. A splash , or two
sprinkled from the falls
a wake-up, a look down
then gone.

The grip
of a hummingbird,
like the kiss of a spiderweb,
so slight, like a wish,
an afterthought.
I won't forget the water --
water for humming birds.

embi 8/16/11

Limits

Dappled sunlight with
so many greens,
I could be
underwater.
Firewood
of seasoned oak,
stacked and standing
sentinel to the boundries
of the deck,
while granting shelter
to the chipmunks,
lizards and spiders.
Yellowed leaves
leaving the trees,
to fall and land
like scattered coins
needing
to be spent.
Soft moving wind
cools my skin
and carries the scent
of rosemary, sage and
orange blossom.
Blond-gold contrasts
with silver-grey:
a dozing yellow lab on
an aged redwood deck.

Our morning
repeat visitor, a young buck,
forages beneath
the avocado trees
with hopes of windfall
or knockdown.
His seeming nonchalance
belies his readiness
to leave. The Labrador's
focus is complete.
The stillness
has a texture like
cobwebs made of glass
holding for an instant
only to vanish in
the crashing
bark and growl from
our dog. Warily
standing his ground,
the buck knows
there is a leash.

embi 6/14/11

Errborne

The hummingbird
chased it's life
into our living room
window.
I held it's beating pulse,
bloodied beak and crooked neck
and laid it in a bed
of Burmese honeysuckle.
Unsure of how to comfort,
knowing death is gathering,
my sadness competes
with the air I breathe.
The rise and fall
of the iridescent greens,
blues and blacks
has me scanning
my imagination
for a miracle.
A tiny featherlite
miracle will do.

When I return
the bird has moved
down.
It's wings outstretched
in a frozen reach
upward.
The magnificent will
to launch itself
aloft once more,
granted death's
appointment.
My awe of such
simple determination
gives me pause
and has me
question
where and when,
my nature,
lost
to logic,
fear and
superstition.

embi 7/4/11

Crystal Ship

(a narrative)

My watch was twelve to four,
noon and midnight twice a day.
Wheel-watch, bow-watch and standby
broke four hours into thirds:
eighty minutes at each station
left me a little room to play
my father's four-string banjo,
ignoring comments overheard.

Eighteen years old and bulletproof,
made of rubber and cement
I assumed that everyone would
at least work at my pace,
when our sledgehammers for pounding rust
would barely make a dent
and the other deckhands yelled at me
"slow down it's not a race".

The "jitterbug" had steel teardrops
mounted on a spindled shaft
driven by a motor loud enough
to deafen anyone's approach.
The Bos'n told me how and where to chip,
dead certain I was daft.
Apparently I proved his point when I learned,
the hard way, how he coached.

I'd chipped the section he'd laid out
and had moved onto the other side.
Now my ears are ringing, my nose is bleeding
and I'm crumpled in a heap,
then my ass starts aching and I'm wonderin
WHAT!, and why the motor died,
while the Bosun's yelling WTF
and should he throw me in the deep.

I was learning that the way I was brought up,
went against the practice set
by the Union protocol. The Bosun's
yelling that I'm taking away work
from tomorrow's planned production.
I'm not supposed to do that yet.
I'd been kicked in the butt, headfirst into a capstan.
I think the Bosun is a jerk.

Our deck cargo was train axles corralled
by 2x10s then cabled to the bulkhead
to keep them stationary when we ran
into high seas. Alfalfa filled the cargo holds,
then our noses, throats and lungs when
the empty holds were cleaned. I dread
the next hold cuz the temp is one hundred
ten degrees: so I'm dreaming about cold.

At sea the routine norm was mornings
chipping paint and afternoons my watch
duties til four and then my time off til midnight
and my watch would start again.
One job was in a bos'n's chair undoing shackles
with the mast against my crotch
high up enough to see the ship's bow
cleaving waves for dolphins playing, then

eye to eye with a pelican winging past
with his catch still kicking in his sack.
At moments like this the vastness and
the glory of the ocean struck me dumb.
The ever changing glitter of the sun
on living water, dancing over and back
with the ship's dip and roll I see across
waves and into depths I'll never plumb.

Sometimes a storm would brace the ship
with power not of man and we would
have to change our routines to make it
through the fury of watery mountains
and valleys slowly climbed and descended
while the wind did what it could
to push me and the rain into stumbling
on the decks against the fountains

surging up and over the ship's bow and
bulwarks. With that much water crashing
on deck, no watch can stand on the bow.
Instead my watch is on the bridge where
I watch for other ships' lights. High above me
the radar tower's red light's flashing.
To my delight the ladder up puts me in
the crows' nest. At first, just standing there

is close to God and magical but slippery
with the rain and wind so I sit on the perch
with my legs between the rails and gloried
in the magnificence. With the pitch and
roll the tower listed starboard and port,
so I hung over roiling water with each lurch.
Side to side a slow ark through gusts of wind
and rain, while lightening split grand

sections of the blackened skies. My suspension
over water boiling cold enough for
hypothermia, while the pulse of the storm
became my heartbeat, my mortal self
let go and drowned in the divine and
for those fragile moments I felt no rebuff or
doubt, just freedom from me. But flashlights
below said I had to abort my shelf.

I climbed down into a fury made of man
this time, they thought I'd washed over-
board or somehow left my post. My claim
that the tower was the best possible
look-out, fell on deaf and angry ears.
My watch did not include a high storm lover.
Regardless, my awe of natures' might
has shown me how quickly we're disposable.

The morning brought us broken clouds
then sunlight and calm waters with a salt
crystal deposit over all the decks,
rails, booms, masts, chains and winch cables.
The sunlight set the salt crystals sparkling,
magically gifting a world without fault.
Until the rains, our crystal ship would
dazzle mornings for as long as she was able.

The gift of nature's yin and yang, her arbitrary
push and pull, or the whim of God,
has humbled me each time I remember
and witness a storm. My lessons continue
with each storm in my life and sometimes
I'm lucky that the occasional odd
epiphany actually remain. Knowing that life
given me is also residing within you,

completes my connection. Our great grey
mother the sea holds us and our planet
together. While at the correct distance
from the sun, we are enabled and able to
acknowledge order beyond our making.
Given my life, I haven't always planned it
but maybe, maybe when my time has come,
I will be remembered as a fable too.

embi 4/27/14

Lace Architecture

Early morning walk
in the oak woods
with the sunrise
on the left, I guess
I'm walking south.
Tar, a black lab, and I
are chasing a sheeps' trail
along the eastern crest
of the ridge. Rounding
the crest, the woods thin,
letting the sunlight
dazzle the dew caught
on the crosswork
of cobwebs strung
a foot above the forest floor.
All along the edge of
that ridge I witnessed
the night time industry
of the spiders' spinning,
glowing like crystals
on the foot high network,
leaving the edge of the forest
sparkling with the sunlit dew.
I don't know if Tar saw
what I saw but he stopped
and sat in the trail
as if he was struck
by the same magic.

We stayed a while like that.
As the sun climbed my back
the view into the forest
floor deepened, lighting
up that glistening grid,
until the jeweled macrame
faded into the shaded woods.
The weather, animals
and man all contribute
to the ruin of the shin
lace architecture.
What I now know is
that the night crew
will build tomorrow
mornings' gleaming
latticework for whomever
chooses that morning walk.

embi 3/31/14

Toodlin'

I rode it on a bet
through the rail-yard
crisscrossed like
tic-tac-toe,
past wondrous
steel sculptures
of wheels, cowcatchers and
smokestacks chugging
their lungs for motivation.

Skeleton steel dinosaurs
dip their heads, feeding
from grain cars
patiently waiting in line
with their offerings.
My articulated carrier
rolls past the bones
of the city and the
ramshackle track shacks
to the countryside
picketed with
telephone lines,
stitching a border
on the yellow-green
fields and blue skyline.

The boxcar's open door
strobes the hammocks,
hills, horses and houses,
with flickering sunset,
distracting from the odor
of penned up sheep.
The hypnotic rumble
and clanging of the
rails and car hitches
lurching and gliding,
gliding and lurching,
provides rhythmic
solace and peace.

Hurtling through space
on the edge of the earth
at 70 miles an hour,
grants an immediate
demand for my complete
self awareness as I
climb the car's sliding
door frame to the
roof of the car to
stand in the wind
as it rips at my hair,
face, chest and legs.
The racing pastel
panorama of the
dusk-drawn suburbs'
first lights, sparkling
on the horizon,
illustrate a vista
strewn with other
living beings.

Climbing down
from the boxcar
to the flatcar up
ahead, the darkening
skies showcase a
stellar canvas hung
with celestial crystals
suspended in transparent
indigo and cobalt.

Lying on my back on
the bed of the flatcar,
feeling the rhythmic
surge of the steel dragon
charging through the
darkening twilight,
I can't help but notice
my immediate velocity
against the slow motion
heavenly bodies.

Especially with the blasting,
gusting, roaring, rattling
air shattering passage
of another steel dragon
in the opposite direction

Slightly shaken but not
stirred, I decide to sit
on the roof of the boxcar.
The wind tears my eyes
as I watch the hi-ways
streaming with headlights
while passing stockyards,
junkyards and backyards,
creek-beds, bay-shore marshes,
concrete aqua-ducts
and overpasses, as
darkness drowns the
twilight, city lights
begin to fill the horizon
causing a cautious
hesitation, a slowing down,
as if the surging dragon
is reluctant to enter the
steel bone yard on the
backside of the city.

Once again the crisscrossed
tic-tac-toe of the rail-yard,
patch-worked in shadows,
of dormant dragons brings
this rolling steel sculpture
to a hissing, screeching halt.
The darkness becomes
my ally as I climb down
to the crushed granite
hoping to avoid arrest
at the hands of the
yard guards.

embi 6/27/14

Redwood Souls

(a sawyer's insight)

The father had some questions,
the mother's smile, pretty with interest,
listened while the daughter hid behind,
sharing her face from time to time.
Our need was to divert the runoff
from the wooded hill behind
their home, whose basement
flooded every winter.

We felled two dozen redwoods,
each close to three feet thick,
once reaching high enough
to capture fog and salty air.
Taking homes from owls,
eagles, hawks, cougars,
bobcats, foxes & raccoons,
left me stunned with sorrow.
I knew we had a job to do,
designed to protect the
family home from nature's
continued resistance,
but at what cost?

As a sawyer my job was to mill:
after bucking these magnificent trees
into twenty foot logs, then
milling them into lumber in order
to build a three hundred foot long
retaining wall a minimum of
three feet in height, using full dimension
two-by-twelves and six-by-sixes.

At first the task seemed straight
forward: leveling and aligning
the mill parallel to a two-story
pyramid of logs backed up
to the forest. However,
as I began to unwrap
these beautiful cylinders,
the richness of the grain
became a beacon of colors
from yellow-gold to rose-pink
to blood-red all glistening with life
and I began to weep.
I was struck by the outrage
of the forest at having
to witness my filleting
their brothers and sisters.
(Redwoods are known for
growing in "families".)

I walked to the edge
of the fading green swale
and knelt, asking forgiveness
and giving thanks for
their majestic bounty.
Each day as I crossed
that marshy meadow
I greeted the woods
asking for their blessing
and forgiveness.

On the days I worked alone
I felt the forest's presence,
as if including and allowing
me and my thoughts.
I was comforted by
the apparent wisdom
garnered over time
by these gentle giants.

The noise of the mill
kept the animals at bay
but when I stopped
for lunch, in the quiet,
I could hear the breath
of the woods and the
sotto voce's crescendo
into a full-voiced symphony.
From the buzz of the bugs
to the chee of the red-tail hawks,
the woodpeckers' percussion,
the chatter of the blue jays.
and the chitter of the
squirrels and chip-monks,
I had the privilege of an
organic orchestra
with my lunch.

The woods began at
the base of the incline and
served as a natural divide
for the wall and "French drain".
The runoff from the hill
that caused the flooding
we hoped to capture and
divert into that drain.
The finished wall began
well past the rear of the house,
ran to the edge of the swale
and in places ran to a
height of five feet.

I cherish my recollections
of that job for several reasons:
the family for whom I worked,
the hard physical labor
my body gifted me and
my sacred relationship
with the redwoods, I can
look back, give thanks
and say "well done".

embi 8/9/14

LOVE & LOSS

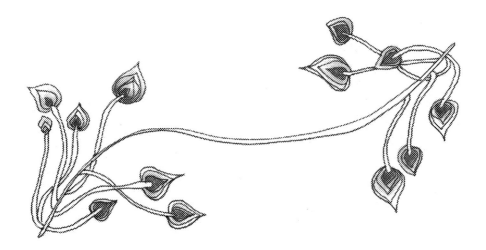

Triage

Three of us on the roof
Sweet William, Camilla and me.
Naive lovers content and spent
on the fringe of society.
Watching the dawn on sidewalks drawn
in shadow and in sun,
the so called straights with
"Don't Be Late," drinking coffee
on the run.

We'd spent the night in Technicolored
states of altered grace,
and watched the morning break in pieces,
some spilling out of place.
The question then became the search
for meaning in a blink,
with each a different noticing
as thoughts became extinct.

A smile of knowing, all at once,
danced across OUR face,
as songs of traffic bounced off walls
into our outer space.
In time's collection we all shared --
not young, not old, nor wise,
just destinies unfulfilled;
our future's in disguise.

We thought we knew what's best for us
and too for ALL mankind.
But the curse of optimism shows
how completely we were blind.
Sweet William died of AIDS, I heard --
his music in the wind.
His music not unlike Sati's.
Can't think what might have been.

Camilla teaches fifth graders
with her own college degree.
She earned it serving old rich men,
their pleasure from her knees.
Her children are HER kids in class,
her own she'll never know,
the price of business in a work
that costs more than it shows.
A classy lady full of grace,
a gift for any man,
gentle, brave, extremely bright;
I guess I'm still a fan.

Me, I've fought my private wars,
some I've even won.
The rest seem less compelling now
or I'm just too tired to run.
My joy was building songs with guys
who liked to harmonize,
except the drummer when he sang,
the melody just died.
So he played his drums, we played guitars,
and sang about our time:
how hip we were; against the war;
at times we found the rhyme.
We got sorta popular;
we played in clubs and halls.
Back stage a kind of battlefield,
each band gearing for its call.
Our music seemed to earn us friends.
Some company we'd keep.
A fun surprise when I'd arrive
waking from my sleep.

Camilla chose to be a friend.
Sweet William hit the road.
With time someday, I hope for peace
and perhaps a lighter load.

embi 7/3/10

Mourning Morning

Mornings are missing I'm sad to declare.
I'd noticed that's so but I wasn't aware
how much you had opened my eyes to this time
when daylight is walking and starting to climb
the limbs of the trees so the birds can converse.
Then my thoughts fly to you with a turn for the worse,
since I notice your breathing and beautiful hair,
and your music when speaking since none of it's there.
I don't think that I'd wanted this time to be shared,
since I've closed myself off, there's no time for despair.

But now that you've shattered the walls of alone,
I'm now taking a look at what makes a home.
The grumps and the giggles and the laundry to do,
something left on the floor like my favorite shoe.
The way I've been living was only for me,
but there's more that can happen, I'm beginning to see,
like breakfast with someone I really adore.
How great that would be cause it changes the chore
to priviledge and pleasure and sharing and fun.
But you've repacked your bags, I'm not sure what I've done.

And you leave in the night with my wish to be well.
I stuff what I'm feeling and with no one to tell
that hope is a drug that hooks me each day,
while I stoically hope that you'd want to stay.
You can stay in your funk, just stay and be here,
I'll just tickle your toes or nibble your ears.
But my feelings are something I've learned to disdain,
so when empty is always, I handle the pain.
But now that the morning has given me pause,
I'm looking at how I might deal with the loss.

You come stay for a moment. We both want it to work,
then the thinking begins and I feel like a jerk
cause I can't give you peace from what I might say
while you struggle with something that sits in our way.
Let's desist with the thinking, just give me your heart,
you have mine and you've had it right from the start.
When I first saw you standing with sweat in your eyes,
and the morning behind you, I thought I would cry
at how pretty you moved when you're just standing still.
A gift to remember. I know that I will.
So maybe with purpose and wisdom and trust,
we could know that our meeting's not simply a bust.

embi 10/12/85

Heroine, Revenge & Other Wishful Thinkings

(for Eryenne)

Her beauty was exquisite, if you ever got the chance,
cold hard lines and attitude did nothing to enhance.
She kept her anger out in front, her reasons were her own.
I'd visit her in spite of words like "I'd rather be alone".
I'd met her when her scholarship was new and magical.
Her singing caused most heads to turn while singing madrigals.
Today the nurses say that time is running out on her.
There's nothing to be done, unless a miracle occurs.
Her HIV was positive, she's tried not to be afraid,
while hyperbole and well-wishing cannot give her aid.

Before the time when AIDS was known, a plague was all we knew.
Her fear was loss of dignity, her options way too few.
She said she caught it from a friend, I knew she popped some pills.
I didn't know she's shooting smack; explains now why she's ill.
Now the price is being paid; it's not just hers alone,
there's those of us left wondering, how do we atone.
Since her mistakes were ours as well, we dodged a bullet then:
a loved one dies while we still live; is it just a chance of when?

My room was on the second floor, hers was on the third.
I'd finally moved from critical; too long it seemed absurd.
I'd wheel my mending pieces to the elevator doors
and wait for it to elevate me up to the next floor.
The jade green of her sunken eyes still sparkled on their own,
her hair, a shade of cinnamon, showed how little it had grown.
When we were young and singing songs of someone else's rhymes,
her laugh surprised the both of us: rare moments out of time.

She lived in terror of her dad since she was eight years old.
Her mother was his punching bag, sometimes knocked out cold.
Then her turn, a different punch, that left her with an ache
she's carried with her ever since: her joy not his to take!
She learned to distrust mostly men; her singing found a break.
When voices harmonized with hers she found she could create
some solace and a place of peace where the world was right again.
Smiles would come, her foot would tap;
no thoughts of life back then.

Now the bed she's lying on seems more alive than her.
When I'd see her eyes open then mine would start to blur.
She's leaving, we both know it now, I'm holding onto air.
I get angry when I realize sometimes life just isn't fair.
I hold her hand, so like a bird, all set to fly away.
I ask if there is anything that she would like to say.
Her smile becomes sardonic when she thinks on what she had.
Then she says she wishes for one last time to fuck her dad.

embi 7/9/10

The Mailbox

Old man at the mailbox,
slightly bent with age,
sifting through the letters,
hoping for a page or two
from his best friend,
the wife he knew.
The passing cars a whisper
of the times they'd take a ride
to quiet places in the woods,
hands held side by side.
That moment's all he's looking for.
Such joy: his life's new bride.
He sees her now and then,
her bonnet loosely tied.
Knowing when she passed
was the moment that he died.
He'll walk back to the house
that used to be a home,
and in the solitary stillness
an unholy lonely tomb
engulfs the empty shadows
as he tours the vacant rooms.
Still he knows that she is waiting
maybe out in the backyard.
He'll hear the water of her laughter,
dog and ball both racing hard
to catch the ball and then return
to her open arms. His vision blurred
by memories and tears that burn,
knowing empty noise is all he heard.

Forgiving her departure seems
like such a futile game.
It doesn't change the emptiness
or even who's to blame.
It begs for some stability
When nothing stays the same
except the hunger of the void,
a hunger he can't tame.
He spends his present in the past;
he's watching yesterday,
choosing moments of the mind,
home movies his own way.
His happiness, a fleeting thought.
He knows he loves a ghost.
When his children come to visit,
he plays the quiet host.
Platitudes and good ideas
scatter in his ears.
His gratitude is make believe.
He is his own worst fear.
Is the answer patience?
Is there really such a thing?
Can meaning show up once or twice
not caring that it brings?
A fragile moment full of life;
the now a constant high.
Gratitude in easy reach,
no questions of the why,
with expectations blown to hell;
the promise now a lie.
If he believed in afterlife,
his path is crystal clear.

But legends, myths and common sense
don't mix unless your fear
of the unknown outweighs
nature's order through the years.
Confounded by his intellect,
adrift with pain and strife,
is the time he spends of better use
moving on beyond this life;
the mailbox's shadow runs southwest;
his shadow's in the light.
I think of him when I drive by;
empty mailbox on the right.

embi 4/27/10

Tormenta de Rayos Lindos

We ended up slow, making love, though it started out as sex.
The Shaman we just visited had left us wanting more.
Our time with him suddenly made life much more complex.
Though your first choice was a woman, you didn't close the door.
Our urgency said take our time, we've not been here before.

The band we played in toured a country alien to us.
The Indian and Cowboy wars would show up time to time.
Sometimes the Cowboys yelled for us to get back on the bus.
But when we played the Rolling Stones,
they thought we played just fine,
while the Indians in the back all stood there in a line.

Our female vocalist stood out not only for her looks,
her family line was Cherokee; her stature a cliché,
but when she sang sometimes you'd see the anger that it took
to make it through another night with a mob that wants its way.
So the cover tunes outnumbered all the songs we'd want to play.

We'd written songs that made us laugh and some that made us cry.
But they were ours, a way to say what mattered to us all.
But to only play the top chart tunes was too much like a lie.
So if our song was anti-war, we'd hear booze and loud catcalls.
Seems sad when happiness looks like a bottle off the wall.

The Indians from the back took us in their jeep.
The two of us not sure what or where we might end up.
At the time we couldn't know how much we'd wreck our sleep.
They took us to their Shaman who gave us each a cup.
We sat, he spoke, we listened til the sun was coming up.

No one spoke on the ride back; there wasn't any need.
The parking lot of the club seemed desolate and bleak.
But the joy cascading from her smile showed part of her was freed.
In quiet dawn at the motel, neither felt the need to speak.
While the morning hours seemed long enough to last us for a week.

We found each other crying in an embrace we understood.
The language uttered through our touch was new and tentative,
and the landscape had us flying without knowing that we could.
The hills and valleys spoke to us; the mesas rose to give
the sound of thunder to the heart -- a sacred place to live.

The lifetime of my time with her; like a whistle in the wind,
you're certain that the notes you heard are what you think they are,
but whistles fade, so do dreams; fond memories come unpinned.
Now the gentle rain that was a storm's been captured in a jar
that lets me sip from time to time as I wonder how you are.

embi 5/25/11

Cotati '66 / What's Left

Your phone call brought a heartache
we each endured alone.
My calls all went unanswered while
I thought you still were home.
When you told me that the doctors
had turned you inside out
and left the early table baby
to perish there without
life or love, enfolded in
the arms of mom or dad,
I died a death that I repeat
when I think of what we had.

I don't have the words to capture
your loss, or even mine;
you made a choice to end it and
we can't go back in time.
If only I'd been there with you,
if just to hold your hand.
It was your decision, I agree:
the act I understand.
But doing it all by yourself,
I weep in my concern.
To share it with me afterwards,
I don't know what we learned.

I ask forgiveness for the loss
of trust, of faith, of life.
The phone call left a searing wound
created by the knife.
I know you had to say the words
so I'd know that they were real.
After all this time it doesn't change
the loss I'm meant to feel.
Giving life, then taking life --
two opposites, at least.
The first, a momentary bliss,
the last, a lifelong beast that
tastes forgiveness with a finger
pointing back at me
and laughs at penance knowing
some truths can't set you free.

embi 4/20/10

Ghost Crop

The tractor sits in the rusted field, the grass and weeds waist high;
it hasn't moved since '69, the last year that they tried.
Vegetables and raspberries grew almost every year.
The farmers' market claimed the berries, the veggies fed the deer.

Best friends, or close enough, when they held each other's thoughts,
so the visit to his best friend's home with flowers that he brought
for the wife, with laughter and a quick embrace,
without knowing loneliness wears a smile on her face.

Three days, maybe four, while the visit seemed at peace,
gave room for walks and quiet talks that gave her some release.
While he framed the door and set the sill, they wandered in the field
or leaned against the tractor's wheel, the ghost crop still concealed.

He went to town for lumber, a few hours at the most.
Coming home he brought the rain, and half a dozen posts.
That evening was a quiet time; they all listened to the rain.
When they said goodnight and went to bed,
his blindness hid their pain.

The next day was a wall of gray, the rain like liquid steel.
The tractor in the meadow you'd have to find by feel.
When the guest was late for breakfast, he went to find out why
and found him on the tractors' seat, rain muffling his cries.

He said that he was homesick and really wanted to go home,
so he left for New York City; once more he was alone.
I miss his singing, his songs were mine,
our songs were touched with pain.
I listen to our songs sometimes and see the tractor in the rain.

embi 3/13/12

Shall We

(high school, the long walk)

I came to the dance looking for you.
But not just at the dance,
there was one other place.
You've haunted my dreams daytime and night,
and it can't just be by chance
that I'm still seeing your face.

The spell of the dream has kept me awake,
and I'm lost without any sleep,
but you're still all that I see.
So close when we pass, our shoulders could touch,
but I'm trapped by the secret I keep
and now it's what's unwinding me.

The bittersweet angst that kisses all thought
and helps to color the light
that serves to capture your stance,
keeps me in shadows both silent and still
where I could hide in the night,
but I came here to the dance.

To harbor a dream so far out of reach
that there's no wind left for the sails,
nor will the calm ever find any peace.
But a storm might forgive complacency's guile
whose want is to have us all fail
while killing off passions' release.

To wait in the wings without putting them on
leaves you with feet on the ground,
but your fate gets left up to chance.
Just crossing the floor to be next to you
can you hear/feel/see my heart pound…
and can I have this next dance?

embi 5/22/11

Two Timer

Time without you moves too slow,
I can't wait for it to pass.
But when I'm with you what I know
is time moves much too fast.

I need a way for time to stop
when you are so close by.
And when you're gone, a different way
that teaches time to fly.

If only there were two of you,
one you could leave here,
then I could study every night
how best to hold you near.

The other one could go on home
to do what you must do,
then every time you went away,
I'd still be holding you.

embi 4/17/63

Bitter-Sweet Excursion

Saturday sidewalk:
kids, dogs, skateboards,
bicycles, packages
and all flavors of folks.
Gourmet coffee
beans and teas,
dress boutiques
and garden supplies,
a bagel shop and a
next door delicatessen.

A world tour of
restaurants to
smell and taste.
All too familiar
for the two of them,
painfully so for one.
Alone in a crowd
of disconnected
people on hi-tech
connections in
one sided speeches
generously shared,
she joins the parade
with her I-Phone
against her ear.

Wanting to share
once more with
her lover, she dials
his phone hoping
his hands can answer.
Hearing his voice,
she starts to share
where she is
while her tears
spill in lines
down her face
So happy to hear
her descriptions
of when they spent
time unencumbered
with care, that at first
he can't hear the
tears in her voice
then he crumbles
with tears of his own.
Together they speak
of the where's
and the when's,
remembering;
together again.

embi 5/18/14

Early Morning Drive To Work

A nailclip of a crescent moon,
a pulltab in the sky,
if we try to pull it open
will it blind our inner eye?

The cold silver of the crescent
impaled on icy blue,
beyond our reach except in dreams,
like the ones I have of you.

embi 6 /27/10

Father's Day

How do her tears reach all the way to my cheeks
when we're just trying to talk on the phone?
She says she's afraid that I'm not gonna return
that I'm not really coming back home.
Whatever assurance I want to provide
gets choked back when I look at the odds,
truth and hope both, seem to argue each day
while fate rides the whim of the gods.
The home that we built with some of our friends
echoes with half of us gone;
holding out for the time when I might return
is something we can't depend on.

Last year, Father's Day was an unconscious affair;
I was a shadow on most people's wall.
My meals through a tube through a hole in my gut;
a catheter to answer the call.
This Father's Day, I got to spend with my wife
and our four legged daughter named Chai,
a truly sweet dog I haven't seen in two years.
My joy and surprise helped me cry.
She's a big yellow lab who never grew up
and her ass wags the edge of the earth.
She loves everyone no matter their mien,
and she's been that way since her birth.

I'm in my wheelchair watching my wife
who weighs in at a hundred plus pounds,
holding the leash, to an eighty pound dog
whose strength is completely unbound.
How she contains the force and the drive
is a feat that leaves me in awe,
tugging the leash Chai half climbs in my lap
pulling my arm with her paw.
My wife's watching me defending myself
from the love of our dog in my face,
remembering when I could play at the beach
while training to keep her in place.

Her watching, I realize, is noticing how
much I have changed this past year.
The arms that I used to hug all I love
can barely reach past my ears.
To reach out and hold what I hold dear
is a dream and a wish I employ.
I miss my arms. Growing up we'd embrace,
so hugging was part of my joy.
Finally accepting the truth of the obvious loss,
her heart is more heavy than gold.
Driving home with our dog, to nobody home
defies her will to grow old.

She calls me to tell me she's gotten home safe
then I hear the fear in her voice.
Is our future on phones and visits to here
all that we have left to rejoice?
The children have grown and have kids of their own
so their father's day is complete.
Their life day to day is full of the gifts
that come when each other's replete.
For us there's a void defined by the words
used to name the disease that I've got,
since no treatment exists for the name that they use
going home becomes probably not.

Still, I have to give thanks to family and friends
who support both me and my wife.
I have to include all my friends on Face Book
cuz you too, are part of my life.
The eternal moments found in the wee hours
would kill without memories of you;
so I rebuild this world with the love you have shown
while I'm wondering how I'll get through
long nights and long days with a few staff who care,
while I watch my faculties fail.
And yet miracles happen, I see them each day,
for my own, who knows what that entails.

embi 6/15/14

OCCASIONAL INSIGHTS

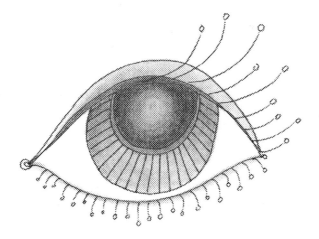

Attendant's Smile

What are you smiling about ?
I said.
I donno, everything? People are funny.
She said.
You mean it's not a nervous tic?
I said.
No people really are funny.
She said.
That's what the head abbot in Thailand said.
I said.
Really, she said that?
She said.
He said.
I said.
Oh, I thought they would have been more enlightened by now.
She said.

embi 8/13/11

Waste Management

The drum-skin sidewalk with it's beat
collides with people's good intents
and spills symphonics in the streets where
the homeless still can't pay their rent.

How much fear is in polite,
is courtesy a sideways dance,
is attitude designed for fights
and true respect a broken lance?

The hustle can't deny the pain of
a handout for a crust of bread,
and cardboard homes street-cleaned each rain,
our culture's gift, the walking dead.

Discarded elders with a home
made by corporate bottom-line,
that leaches souls from living tombs
with bland and safe and tasteless wine.

Do dollars make us worthy folk,
so the law protects our greed?
Your casket might be made of oak,
but the worms still have to feed.

Our café culture's looking good,
in hopes it will be seen
kissing ass and laughing,
should the joke be less obscene than

the price of petrol for the poor,
the rich don't give a damn.
The scraps that get left on the floor
would feed a hungry man.

Where have we gone that prison walls
are designed for our return,
while higher learning's hallowed halls
can't afford to have you learn.

It isn't what you know but who,
and have you greased their plate?
Not caring who you stick it to,
hoping payback will be late.

When greed becomes a culture's choice
and no one uses common sense,
then listening hears the loudest voice
and decency becomes pretense.

The richest mines are taxpayers;
we've seen that since the time of kings,
and ideas like democracy
were songs, as children, we would sing.

With congress as our lawmaker,
designed by trust of corporate greed,
while senators choose to raise their pay
but not for those on whom they feed.

We're lost without a telephone
and television feeds a lust,
while automakers throw us bones
that promise thrift, expecting trust.

We've driven past where our return
could save our children's peace of mind,
while we sit and watch our planet burn,
hoping the gods will be more kind.

The mortal wounds of this blue sphere,
where the living worships ritualized death
instead of life that once was dear,
tells us change too late won't change what's left.

embi 3/20/11

Brainflee

An idea, not unlike a fleabite on the brain,
wants to be scratched from time to time.
Some persist, some flow right down the drain,
some provoke behavior others call a crime
mocking efforts, chasing skittish words,
like trying to catch water with your hands
or keeping jackrabbits gathered in a herd.
Those changes won't help challenge where I stand.

Standing on an effort sounds like leaving in a huff.
Is that four-wheel drive or public transport?
While you're at it, don't forget to take your stuff,
but then some of your ideas you simply just abort;
writing to be writing, a self indulgent way to spill
whatever's held internal to exposure to the light,
while order appears random and chaos always will,
still ricochets of common sense are begging for a fight.

Weighty thoughts and acid reign and "hey, that's heavy man",
the sound of colors running free against my window's pain
while truth collides with Sunday School revealing man/gods' plan,
and tickets bound for heaven's gate cost more than the whole train.
So people get ready! But the train is for the rich! Maybe there's a bus
to catch like a cold or measles, (I forgot, the rich ride planes
so who rides trains?) the still employed?, unlike the rest of us.
It's not just me. The rules have changed. The whole world's gone
insane.

embi 9/20/11

Silhouette

He took his time and then left,
not so neatly rolled or folded,
more like worn out, colors all bereft.
It was his, after all, to take,
though others borrowed time to time,
leaving moments in his wake.

The gift of time he carried
in his bag of skin and bones,
so that the parcel could be ferried
thought-to-thought as if owned,
through inference, by that piece of time
used randomly -- all reason still unknown.

The pulse of life apparent
in the silhouette we offer
becomes a memory inherent with
encounters caught and postured,
then collected for the files
of our mental storage locker.

The envelope of time we're let
sometimes shows it's wear and tear
when thinking on the chance we get
to bring our unique soul to bear.
In spite of all the times we've bet,
the universe simply won't care.

His fear of passing, not unlike the wind,
comes and goes with purpose or without,
still looking for a way to help rescind
the verdict he knows hardly anything about.
Yet the more he knows suggests he pull the pin
when he can't be heard unless he has to shout.

Left alone the mark can plainly see
the space that's almost always left behind,
and wonders if that moment is what frees
itself. Or does it just simply help remind
us that our fate is carried in the breeze,
a kite set free…while the string unwinds.

embi 3/26/12

Finding Richard

Peering over the curvature
of the earth,
I should say my belly,
my Richard seems so small
and far away.
I recognize that
my eyesight
is diminished,
so glasses, where
are my glasses?
Now memory, now.
Where's my memory?
Where's my vision?
Where's my Richard?
He's been hiding
in the underbelly
alone, malnourished
and neglected.
Will the real Richard
please stand up?
I run my hands
through my hair,
my glasses bounce
into soapy water.
There they were,
on my head in order
to wash my face.
I can see clearly now
that my faraway
Richard was really
my big toe.

embi 4/19/11

Snowbound

Awake and alone
in a settling house,
enveloped by snow and blue ice
that blankets the roof,
and the hills and the trees;
how can such cold look so nice?

A white wind, while walking,
stealing the heat from my body,
doesn't care about dreams for tomorrow.
While a break in the flurry
offers crystalline starlight,
and a stillness I only can borrow.

A still moment frozen
with you on my mind,
then the hurry of looking for cover.
Icicles gleaming
like lances of silver,
reflecting the smile of your lover.

To delight in the beauty
of this soft quiet whiteness
without you to laugh in the snow,
reminds me you're missing
with your work never ending
and places we don't seem to go.

Is my worth as a husband
just measured in dollars?
Are dreams worth a handful of sweat?
Moving mountains or molehills
that happen in moments
with our future a worry still yet.

Until something changes,
little by little,
there's nothing to show of the dream.
Remembering wishes
can sometimes be painful
like the snowflakes that smother my screams.

Making most of the moment
while time hangs remorseless
on shoulders too weary to care,
and the burden of caring
for each other's wishes
still happens when nobody's there.
So if we go missing
while sitting together, MAYBE
it's time we got out of our chairs!

embi 2/25/11

The Beauty of False Hope

Too late to change it, too late to save it,
too late to say goodbye.
And leaving is too painful,
while staying holds us captive
where we're barely held together
in this frightful lullaby.

If you don't have the answers, I won't ask the questions.
So we're stuck together, wondering about why.
But knowing why won't matter, our truths are others' ashes.
While death defines an ending, still the living barter
about who else can afford the right to die.

Love and loss are equals, each bound in time together
without the choice of when it has to end.
While you're dancing in the ether, our lives stay in the struggle,
not knowing how much time is spent
just trying to make amends.

How delicious is a heartache, is it worthy of forever,
does "noble" really help to set a trend?
If my waking after dreaming chases echoes with a skateboard,
and finds storm clouds caught in fishnets with the moon,
then I find that trust is useless as long as we won't listen,
cause it seems as if we'd rather just pretend.

Do dreams all lose their magic when children become cynics,
and ridicule becomes a special gift
that says how much you love me by how much you help to hurt me?
Maybe losing something special
could at least help teach us thrift.

If fear's what holds us captive, then love enables wisdom;
still my thumb's out asking for a lift.
An open door may save us, but the ride won't wait to claim us.
If the sands are running out, and time is bankrupt,
I wonder what's been left for us to sift.

embi 2/12/12

Intro & Circum

Writing on empty, going nowhere not so fast,
wondering what to write about, I haven't got a clue.
With nothing in the thought pantry, how long's it going to last,
I keep hoping some insight might arrive out of the blue.
When the vehicle I'm writing seems completely out of gas,
and new ideas so far away a jet can't get me there,
I'm learning now that waiting doesn't mean "this too will pass"
and thoughts occur ready or not from incredibly thin air.
My need to write a masterpiece, whether a thousand words or nine,
digs at me when not writing and haunts me when I am.
To come up with a stirring phrase that grips the heart and mind,
and opens doors to thoughtfulness, and know we give a damn.

The notion that there's nothing to believe or even trust
means I've lost the faith or given up or quit on chasing good,
except I can't help think my children, who are worthy, kind and just,
are trapped inside the world I leave where the heroes all once stood
for decency towards all the poor, the have-nots and the lame --
for teachers, rabbis, imams, and poets, librarians and cops,
for truckdrivers and carpenters, they're all part of the game,
for bartenders and firemen who don't know when to stop,
and all the others left at risk, we stood for them as well.

Now it seems our policies are made from greed and fear --
designed to change our judgments like on the priests from hell,
or the fear of equal rights for those whose thoughts are just as dear
to them as ours to us, though they speak a different tongue,
or love their love, their fellow man as if they are a wife,
or the God they see at worship has a different sound when sung.
When did we stop embracing the differences in life?

embi 6/25/11

Petroglyphs

(comments from the cave)

To live a lie successfully,
you have to tell the truth --
at least a little, time to time,
the rest would be uncouth.

When whole truths show a sadder shape
at least in our own eyes,
we've chosen life with prison walls --
freedom's farce a poor disguise.

We promise every good idea
as if we can make it real;
instead, depression and disgust
maintain the right to steal

our laughter and our sense of self
held hostage by each failure's weight;
the wins discounted or forgot
or seen as just a lucky break.

Our love of falling fascinates
our view of the abyss.
Is self-destruction easier?
Is life a gift dismissed?

embi 3/8/11

I Lost My Song

I had a freedom high or low
without regard for how.
The sudden urge to recreate
provokes me even now.
What I know is, currently,
the noise I make is raw,
and leaves me empty, not unlike
a man made out of straw.

To take for granted nature's gifts
is arrogant and blind.
Two frequent places in my life,
not too hard to find.
Unaware it was unique,
a scholarship was won.
But singing was a natural act,
something done for fun.
To "study voice", what does that mean,
is science part of this?
I thought the heart of what I did was
uncomplicated bliss.

To play and sing just for fun,
while the only need was rent;
money wasn't why we played,
though it was always spent.
The MUSIC was the why of things;
our POEMS were given sound,
and pulse and energy,
while restrictions came unbound.

I just sang. When people smiled,
the world fell into place.
To open up in public
without regard for space,
and stand beside another voice,
in the gift of harmony.
Freedom's when the audience
is just like you and me,
while playing at the Fillmore
or the Avalon Ballroom,
their upturned faces, body gyrations
and groupies in mid-swoon.

What we did was sought after,
made O.K. by choice;
our following was part of us,
it too had a voice.
The simple joy of singing songs
made by our own hand,
gave us a place where we were heard
outside of just the band.

I hear parts of what once was
on records, tapes and discs:
memories of a time I never
thought I'd miss.
Today it seems that yesterday
had meaning, choice and hope --
all clichés you often hear
when you're simply trying to cope.

embi 8/12/11

Not So 'lever

what happens
when I run
out of clever,
and beauty takes
a backseat
while grace
tries to board
a dugout
canoe?
is my stream
of consciousness
a babbling brook,
or up a creek,
riding the rapids
to an ocean
of elusive ideas
or, more likely, just
a leaky faucet?
waiting for inspiration
is like chasing
wishful thinking
with a tennis racquet.
to try keeping clever
thoughts is not
unlike holding
boiling water in
a balloon.
when I heard
"go soak your head"
I didn't know
drowning in ideas
meant swimming
in a sea of
meaninglessness.   embi 7/8/11

PORTRAITS

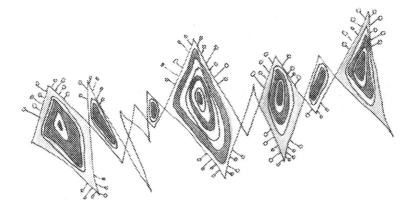

Twice a Graveyard

(the discovery of bird bones in an abandoned nest,
while dismantling a steel Quonset hut)

Iron behemoth,
tin hide skinned,
insides pinned with girdered steel.
Her metal beams embraced a nest.
A steel cradle blessed with
bones of rust, staid and trussed,
now a skeleton. Dust,
fine and complete,
over bleached white lace.
A last resting place
free of body meat.
Nuts and bolts scattered
no longer matter.

embi 6/14/ 66

Vanishing Prairie

(WAKING FROM A DREAM)

The burnished yellow grass of the sun-
parched prairie, brittle and broken
by the wind, platters up a solitary rider.
Still as ice, he's fastened to the horizon
by ebony eyes seeking sustenance
for his family and his people.

At the edge, the seam, the crack where
the periwinkle blue and the chrome yellow
join, comes a speck, a dot, a fractured movement.
Against the brassy glare the blackened silhouette
wavers like a mirage, a glistening ripple
gaining mass, heartbeat by heartbeat.

Still, eternally still, the rider breathes
with the breeze and buzz of the insects.
Can life be coming? Will talking stomachs
be silenced? Are there skins for clothing
and shelter, gut for bowstrings, horn for blades
and greasy smiles for the children?

The speck is now a shape, a thing that can
be known. A buffalo, the leader of a herd?
The creature's size and shape can be defined. And yet,
the empty space behind the bison steals the heart.
The wind does not carry the smells or sounds
of the rest of the herd. Eternity on the horizon.

The Tatanka are missing. Where are the others?
As a boy, the bison were as an ocean,
filling the prairie with hooves, horn, muscle and fur.
The hunt took the whole tribe into action
from cooking pots to sharpened lances.
Each person eager to give to the hunt.

The lone rider, known to his people as Red Wolf,
studies Tatanka's approach. As the distance behind
becomes a distance beyond, Red Wolf's despair
all but consumes his purpose. The magnificent
animal forages ahead on a return journey,
he too, looking for more of his kind.

Red Wolf can't help but notice the scars
and the bull's arrhythmic gait from a wound
on his hip. The dried blood, a muddy brown,
shows where a not so old bullet still lodges.
"Where are your people?" calls out Red Wolf.
"The long rifles take us," replies Tatanka.

"I have come for you," declares Red Wolf.
"That I know and welcome. I find no honor
in the long distance death," replies Tatanka.
"But I will not be the one who takes the last
of your people," states Red Wolf. " My time
is past, as yours follows," replies Tatanka.

Saddened by the truth, Red Wolf turns away,
leaving the noble beast to his life and dreams.
As he rides toward the mountains, thinking
of his family, he does not hear the bullet
that passes through his heart and out his chest,
his riderless horse heading, at last, for home.

embi 9/24/11

Skid Marks and Road Kill

Grandfather came to hold his son
since the son can't embrace his;
the grandson left to hang with friends
and take care of his own biz.

The son's garage is busy now,
grandfather holds a wrench.
The banner on the wall reminds
while my tire's on the bench.

That morning as I drove to work,
the sheriff stopped the cars
and the CHP offered turnarounds,
time or distance just as far.

A mom came running up the street,
then landed on her knees.
The sherriff kneeled to gather her;
the truth denied her pleas.

Tire burns across the road,
then gouges in the rough.
Metal stuck, left in the tree,
shows the car was fast enough.

Leaving the bodies bent and broken,
now lost their chance at life,
accelerations' thrill of speed
ripped through them like a knife.

A tribute to the three dead youths
I witness every day
as I drive by the hillock where
the scarred tree stands and sways.

To lose a son, an awful phrase,
a fear throughout my days.
My mother's faith I borrow,
at times it almost stays.

No way for me to know his loss –
to honor the grandpa.
Though my tires help to keep me safe,
they can't alter what I saw.

embi 3/20/11

Our Lady of the Crosswalk

She stops traffic with her smile.
The children wait a while
til it's safe to reach the middle
where She stands.
Our Lady of the Crosswalk
holds the cars and trucks in small talk
with the children holding
drawings, toys and hands.

They can't wait to see her,
to touch, to catch and greet her
with their Paris-plaster cups
or their stories of their pups.
When she listens,
we all know how much she cares.
From the window of my car
I can't help but think how far
it is from here
to conversations playing over there.

I want the gladness and the joy.
I want to be a boy again
and have her hold my hand
to cross the street.
Our Lady of the Crosswalk
is the heartbeat of the school block.
Would that the blessing of our passage
be as sweet.

embi 2/17/11

Moving Window

I like this older couple, every morning with their dog.
Tennies, coats, a headlamp, breaking through the fog.
One's on the leash, one's on the light, maybe they trade at home.
Still, they're out there every morning and I've yet to see a phone.
Maybe they're old fashioned; maybe time's a different weight.
Agendas for the future not so easy to relate.
When every day is precious with the wonder at the dawn,
and the movement in the bones reminds us time moves on
without our help or hindrance; we're just lucky for the ride.
I notice time's indifference seems to take us all in stride.
I motor by and realize I want to walk with them.
I've made up who they might be, I know it's all pretend.
If I stop and ask a question is there time to make new friends?
I wonder where they're going; is it home or work or play?
If home, is the house empty, do the children stay away?
Or is there joy and laughter soaked in the floors and walls,
with momentary sadness like when a grandchild falls?
Do they work the in-home office replete with hi-tech toys,
trading off to work the garden when they need a different ploy.
Or, are they both retired, content with reading books,
a little sherry in the evening while deciding who's to cook?
Maybe they set the table to include an extra place
in case chance offers someone who's willing to share grace.

So, they're different in their ways, with time spent in the closet.
They might have things to say about our culture's laws that
teach division, hate and fear, and bring us all to tears.
Is saying live-and-let-live only true if we're the same?
If your beliefs and mine don't match, is someone else to blame?
These gentle men have found some peace,
a home where ex-wives land,
then take off after visiting still trying to understand.
Yet knowing love has different homes,
and hearts have different minds,
let's stop and take the time to share, we know it takes all kinds.

embi 6/10/10

Make Beleaf

I watched it fall
and in the watching,
time
took its own time.
I saw the rusted
reds and yellow-greens,
and wondered at
the life
of a leaf
that begins with the
hydraulics of
spring --
pushing buds
to the surface.
Day or night
makes no difference
to the unfurling
sails in the sunset
or the chill of dawn.

Summer winds and
sunlight,
paper-water rustling
in the branches,
winged notes rise
and fall from
nests and limbs.
Furry flurries gather
winter stores,
springing
branch to branch,
leaf to leaf.

Do they know
their neighbors?
Are they glad for
the shade in August,
or the colors of
the Fall?
The ground now
a cradle of color
each leaf like a torch:
the fire of
Autumn found
once a year,
each one more
splendid.

From piles built
to scatter,
spilling children,
dogs and laughter;
finally put to flame,
leaving ashes
to feed the new
life of a leaf.

embi 5/17/10 & 7/11/11

Reflections

The startled old man in the mirror
is not the young man in the mind.
The man in the mind is carefree,
that playground he still hopes to find.

The wrinkled old man in the mirror
sees the days melt away with his tears;
remembering people and places
that time has kept hidden for years.

His children don't need him for answers;
their questions address different times.
The grandkids are too busy texting
and they could care less about rhymes.

What he sees are unreachable endings
that outdistance the range of his dreams,
each one laden with great expectations
that time's torn apart at the seams.

While witnessing time's own indifference
whose passage you pay with your life,
so what's precious gets left in the attic
in the mirror left there by the wife.

The quilt of his memory has patches,
some better some worse for the wear,
though the fabric is worn and in pieces
that regrets can never repair.

His pockets are fat with the moments
that mean something special to him,
so he stands with his hands in his pockets
full of marbles and kite-string and whims.

Out of place with cloud memory and i-pads,
back to roads without pavement or cars,
and a tree with a swing and his own dad,
both lost in the light of the stars.

The child in the air is ecstatic,
first earth fall, then the push at the sky;
for the father, pendulums swing both ways,
while the child's just learning to fly.

embi 9/6/11

Thumbs Up

When Tibet was invaded with the intent to destroy
everything their faith and belief systems held,
a sport was devised by the soldiers called pruning.
The purpose: to stop the monks' practice of rolling the thumb
and forefinger over to the next prayer bead.
Using pruning shears, the thumb was removed.
Not having been subjected to that horror, degradation,
and pain, I can only distantly relate to the loss of thumbs.
With the invasion of this current malady, I've noticed
difficulty with my thumbs. For example, I can
no longer hold a chord on the neck of a guitar.
I have difficulty buttoning and unbuttoning, more
especially dire if I have to pee and can't undo my britches.
Holding a cup of coffee seems like a simple task.
Task? It should be simple, but as the cup begins
to tilt away from me, and I tighten my grip and
nothing happens, I might begin to be concerned…
and grateful there was nothing in the cup.

embi 6/5/12

Movin' On

The summit store by five o four
first light on an open road.
A welcome freedom; no one else,
clear lanes and a truck's full load.

Runnin' with the hum and pulse
the truck, the road, the speed,
feels good just to let it roll
headlights are all I need.

Movin' through the tunnel's well
night rounding out the sides,
listening to the road dictate
the rythmn of the ride.

Haulin' freight from town to town,
too soon they're all the same,
lookin' ahead to rhubarb pie
and that waitress, What's Her Name?

Ah yes, Rebecca, I saw her last
with both her arms stacked full
while laughing with a customer;
her smile, my heart, the pull.

She's got three kids, a dog, a cat
and a husband at home, drunk.
Her pretty face, a purple eye,
I'd love to hurt the punk.

My job won't let me get involved,
my heart sez "see what breaks".
Her friendliness belies the weary
cost of what it takes

to wake up every morning tired
beyond her thirty years.
To see hope from a stranger's eyes
gives pause, and sometimes tears.

Everyone in town knows how
bad he treats his wife
yet no one speaks the truth out loud
gossip's just a way of life.

Rhubarb pie and coffee black,
I stare into my cup.
My rig outside has miles to go.
Guess it's time to saddle up.

embi 5/25/10

Rubber Ducky

The exhausted tsunami
pushed the last
wave and rippled
across the entire
San Francisco Bay,
not to mention
the Pacific Ocean,
after wreaking havoc
on a nation
that prepared
its buildings
and its power
on the known but
not the unknown.
Imagination maybe,
if foreseen from
an awful indifference.
No man can truly
grasp, when nature
goes out hunting,
that our numbers
and our habits are
nature's bitter foes.

When the atom left
the castle and roamed,
unchaperoned,
across the countryside;
once again
the people witness
a sixty-six year old
man-eating dragon.
What makes today
seem different?
Is contamination global,
and to condemn a nation
useful?
If the ripple in our
bathtub continues
in this manner,
it won't matter if
there's enough for everyone
when enough is isotopic.
Our world was
so much bigger then;
we're smaller
than that now.

embi 4/12/11

ABOUT THE AUTHOR

I have lived a varied and unique life.

My current wife (June) and I married twenty-two years ago, shortly after I moved to Santa Cruz. Without her I wouldn't be here.

Over two years ago I was diagnosed with ALS, Lou Gehrig's Disease.

The year before that I had retired from my professional endeavors that included fifteen years as a general contractor/sawyer. I took my sawmill to homeowners who wanted to harvest their own timber, milled the logs and built the add on, e.g., barn, deck/trellis etc.

Before that I was a chef in a small French restaurant for five years, in a town south of Santa Cruz by ten minutes or so.

Prior to that I had a spa on the Berkeley/Oakland border on College Avenue, in collaboration with the National Holistic Institute's graduate program. I graduated as an Holistic Health Practitioner and bought the spa. The spa allowed graduates of the Institute to fulfill their hours providing massages at a very favorable discount to the public. For me it was a four year period of personal therapy, recovering from a failed first marriage of twenty years that included two unique and wonderful children.

Before that, I was Maître D'/partner of The BayWolf Restaurant in Oakland where my first wife and I worked for almost ten years. My so called "experience" came from a year at Chez Panisse, in Berkeley, and a year as a cook at El Charro, a Mexican restaurant in Castro Valley.

My previous "career" consisted of three years as a cast member of the rock musical "Hair" and a year at The American Conservatory Theater doing a musical version of "The Selling of the President."

My "musical" link started with a voice scholarship at San Francisco State for three years where I met the mother of our children. I had been playing coffee houses and clubs as a folksinger but McGuinn of the "Byrds" convinced me that Dylan was right about rock and roll, so not too much later I was a member of a folkrock band called "The WildFlower." We became part of the '60s rock scene for three or four years playing the Fillmore Auditorium, the Avalon Ballroom, the Matrix, The Family Dog and the Red Dog Saloon in Nevada, as well as touring western Canada with the "YoungBloods." Our recording contract came through right after the band broke up, of course. My experiences in this era included all of the rich color of a '60s rock and roll lifestyle.

I even spent a year as a merchant seaman after graduating from high school.

All of these many careers, journeys and experiences are played out in my poems, songs and prose.

embi 5/1/14

Michael's music CD, "Greywolf," can be ordered online at:

http://www.cdbaby.com/cd/michaelbenjaminbrown